Living *with* Grief

Living *with* Grief

MINDFUL MEDITATIONS
AND SELF-CARE STRATEGIES
FOR NAVIGATING LOSS

heather stang

CICO BOOKS

LONDON NEW YORK

This edition published in 2024 by CICO Books
An imprint of Ryland Peters & Small Ltd

20–21 Jockey's Fields   341 E 116th St
London WC1R 4BW   New York, NY 10029

www.rylandpeters.com

First published in 2014 as *Mindfulness and Grief*

10 9 8 7 6 5 4 3 2 1

Text © Heather Stang 2014, 2024
Design © CICO Books 2014, 2024

A CIP catalog record for this book is available from the Library of Congress and the British Library.

ISBN: 978-1-80065-307-8

Printed in China

Editor: Rosie Lewis
Designers: Emily Breen and Geoff Borin

CONTENTS

In loving memory of Don, Doug, & Tom

Allow

There is no controlling life.
Try corralling a lightning bolt,
containing a tornado. Dam a
stream and it will create a new
channel. Resist, and the tide
will sweep you off your feet.
Allow, and grace will carry
you to higher ground. The only
safety lies in letting it all in—
the wild with the weak; fear,
fantasies, failures and success.
When loss rips off the doors of
the heart, or sadness veils your
vision with despair, practice
becomes simply bearing the truth.
In the choice to let go of your
known way of being, the whole
world is revealed to your new eyes.

Danna Faulds, from *Go In and In: Poems from the Heart of Yoga*

INTRODUCTION

HOW TO LIVE WITH GRIEF

You have made a wise choice in opening this book. Even though you are grieving, anticipating a loss, or supporting others through such challenges, you have consciously reached for this guide. Your decision to delve into this journey showcases both courage and vulnerability—two essential ingredients in the recipe of resilience.

Perhaps you are curious not only about surviving grief, but how to understand it, coexist with it, and ultimately, continue living—fully, actively, meaningfully—in its presence. Your choice underscores a powerful truth: grief, while painful, does not preclude a life of purpose, connection, and even joy.

If you are in the throes of raw grief, and the idea of living fully with your loss feels unattainable, this book is for you too. The first three chapters will help you tend to acute pain. If you bought this book feeling a sense of optimism, but that spark has since flickered and dimmed, this book is still for you. Living with grief is not a linear journey. It is an ever-changing landscape, with peaks of clarity and valleys of confusion, all undulating with the ebb and flow of emotions. Some days may feel more overwhelming than others but remember; that is okay, and it is a normal, human experience of loss.

POSTTRAUMATIC GROWTH

If you feel skeptical and wonder if surviving grief is even possible, I assure you it is. I have worked with thousands of people in private sessions and support groups, in person and online. I meet most of my clients when the pain is fresh and raw. I am often asked how I can bear to witness this kind of suffering day after day. My answer is simple: I get to see the pain of loss change people in miraculous ways.

This is not some form of toxic positivity—that cringy tendency to overlook, belittle, or invalidate authentic human emotions such as grief, anger, regret, fear, anxiety, or shame. While positive emotions can be skillfully employed when they are genuine, they can also be harmful when forced, or when used to avoid or suppress real feelings that need acknowledgment and processing.

Personally, I do not regard my grief as a gift. If that were the case, I would gladly return this unwanted present in exchange for my loved ones—restored to a state of happiness and health—in an instant. But, given the reality of our losses, many grieving people report a positive, if uninvited, transformation.

The undeniable truth is that grief reshapes you, molding you into a different version of yourself. This transformation, not wished for but inevitable, contributes to what researchers Laurence G. Calhoun and Richard G. Tedeschi at the University of North Carolina, Charlotte, call "posttraumatic growth." This term describes the beneficial changes and aspects of personal growth that follow any significant life event (grief included) that disrupts our emotional equilibrium and challenges our existing beliefs and personal narratives. I think of this as an awakening.

In describing the beneficial aspects of posttraumatic growth, the researchers do not imply that trauma is to be sought after or minimized—it is not toxic positivity. Acknowledging posttraumatic growth is simply to recognize that positive change can emerge from traumatic experiences. There are five key elements that constitute posttraumatic growth, as outlined by Calhoun and Tedeschi:

- Appreciation of life and everyday moments
- Improved relationships with others (I also add with Self)
- Sense of new possibilities in lifestyle and interests
- Increased personal strength and self-reliance
- Spiritual change or growth.

GRIEVING YOUR WAY

This book is not about prescribing a singular "right" way to navigate grief. Such a thing simply does not exist. Modern grief research, or thanatology, recognizes this, even if popular culture has yet to catch up. The chapters in this book outline what I call the "Mindfulness and Grief System," an approach that teaches you how to live with loss.

You will find numerous practices here—some will resonate deeply, while others may not. Encountering a practice that does not click can be an opportunity for self-reflection. Is it uncomfortable because it is challenging, pressing on a raw part of your grief? Or does it simply not align with your personal journey? Sometimes what we resist most can offer the deepest healing, yet it is equally important to recognize not all practices are suitable for everyone—and that is perfectly fine.

Honor your feelings, instincts, and pace. Remember, this is your journey. If a particular practice doesn't suit you, that does not mean you are "doing grief wrong". It simply means that there are tools and methods better suited to your needs and experiences. Be patient with yourself and keep exploring.

YOUR RESILIENCE TOOLKIT

This guide contains the self-care practices and coping skills that I teach my clients and use myself. I include meditation, mindful movement (yoga), and journaling, as well as a few creative expression exercises.

SELF-CARE: THE BEDROCK OF RESILIENCE

Self-care practices aim to replenish your body and mind, laying a strong groundwork for your journey through grief. They help to build a supportive environment conducive to healing and growth. It is the act of showing up for yourself consistently, offering nourishment to your body, and kindness to your mind and heart.

Planning self-care can feel like a lot when you are already feeling overwhelmed. Maybe you think you do not have the time, the energy, or even that you are not worth it. So here is a simple hack: pick one exercise from the book and give yourself permission to start with just five minutes a day for one week. That's it! You are not allowed to do more, even if you want to. Start with baby steps and see where it takes you.

COPING SKILLS: YOUR LIFELINE IN STORMY SEAS

Coping skills are like a life jacket you can reach for when tossed into turbulent and emotional waters. They are the immediate, on-the-spot strategies that help you turn down the volume in stressful situations and calm intense emotions. While self-care practices help build resilience over time, coping skills provide immediate relief in moments of distress. They help us regain our equilibrium and offer a moment of respite from the throes of emotional pain.

You may not always remember to use your coping skills in the heat of the moment, and that is okay. Grief has a way of clouding our minds and sometimes we may simply forget. When you do remember, take a moment to celebrate this victory, however small it may seem. Over time it will become second nature.

THE ROLE OF MINDFULNESS

Mindfulness and meditation serve as the common thread binding these practices. They infuse each element of self-care and coping with a deeper level of awareness. As you embrace mindfulness, you foster a kinder and more compassionate relationship with your grief.

Mindfulness and grief contain the seeds of transformation. Grief forces you to change by assigning you unexpected roles, removing the physical, emotional, and material resources you once had, and changing your assumptive world into an unfamiliar landscape.

Mindfulness allows you to make the most of this new territory by introducing you to the self you are in the process of becoming through your senses. As you reacquaint yourself with your spirit by slowing down and turning your focus inward, you will hear the whispered wisdom of your true self, which has long been forgotten and can now be remembered.

HOW TO USE THIS BOOK

Each chapter in this book includes supportive meditation and journaling exercises. I have included suggested practice times for each exercise but do what works best for you. A personal daylong retreat is also included between Lesson 4 and Lesson 5. You can move through the book sequentially or jump to a lesson that feels like what you need. It is helpful to read through each exercise once or twice before you try it for the first time. Key exercises are available for download at mindfulnessandgrief.com/living-with-grief.

BOWING TO ANCIENT WISDOM

You do not need to be a Buddhist or Yogi to benefit from mindfulness, as the wisdom of these teachings transcends boundaries and enriches lives universally. I did not invent mindfulness or yoga for grief. My simple contribution is to pair these ancient practices with modern thanatology.

The rich cultures that inform this book—Buddhist and Hindu—are two that I deeply respect and benefit from myself. I offer 10,000 bows of gratitude to the sages, teachers, and practitioners who have passed on this wisdom. May these teachings benefit all beings and help reduce suffering.

A NOD TO MINDFULNESS AND GRIEF

This book is an updated version of *Mindfulness and Grief* and replaces the eight-week plan with an eight-lesson format to eliminate any confusion about a timeframe for coping with grief. It does contain the same eight themes that are the foundation of the Mindfulness and Grief System, a technique featured in *The Handbook of Grief Therapies* (2023) and my guided journal, *From Grief to Peace* (2021). While many hospices, grief counselors, yoga therapists, and meditation instructors choose to lead this as an eight-week course, this book offers the opportunity to progress at your own pace.

MY ASPIRATION FOR YOU

Grief isn't something that can be fixed; it is a reality you learn to live with. It invites you to develop self-care habits, rely on healthy coping skills, and connect with people who can lend support or sit with you in silence. Grieving in a mindful way is a nuanced shift in perspective, one that takes time and patience, but that will transform the way you relate to your loss and to yourself.

It is my intention that this guide will feel like a wise and compassionate friend. May these practices be a place you can call home for the rest of your life, and to which you will be able to return again and again to grieve, to love, to celebrate, and to heal. The next time your world is uprooted, you will know you have what it takes not only to survive, but also to live and love again.

With loving-kindness,
Heather Stang, M.A., C.A.

LESSON 1
MINDFUL
AWARENESS

EQUANIMITY THROUGH THE STORM
AND BEYOND

When the heart grieves over what it has lost,
The spirit rejoices over what it has left.

SUFI EPIGRAM

MINDFULNESS AND GRIEF

When you are overwhelmed by grief, mindfulness will help you cultivate equanimity—a calm and steady mind—even as painful emotions arise. Rather than avoiding or compounding what you feel, mindfulness is the practice that allows you to honor your grief as a natural response to love and loss, and frees you from self-criticism or shame. As you learn to be patient and kind to yourself, you will become more able to tap into your resilience during challenging times. Through the lens of mindfulness, the storm of grief becomes less overwhelming as you learn how to expand your view. It's like wiping a foggy window to see clearly outside. You find there's not just grief, but love too. With each breath you take, you can say "Yes, I'm grieving, but that's not all there is to me."

UNDERSTANDING MINDFULNESS

On the first day of the Teaching Advanced Meditation Techniques program at the Kripalu Center, our teacher Sudhir Jonathan Foust illustrated a simple yet poignant definition of mindfulness originally described by Chogyam Trungpa. He drew what looked like the letter V, but more open and with curvy sides. "What's this?" he asked. We all agreed it must be a bird, and eagerly shouted out our response. He smiled and paused for a moment.

"Sky, with bird," he said.

That is mindfulness. It's about observing the sky and the bird equally, without any urge to alter either. When you apply this mindfulness principle to grief, you are able to fully observe your experience: your heartache, love, fear, anger, appreciation for the friend who brought a casserole, and anything else that arrives at your door.

Mindfulness is comprehensive, and it shifts your perspective from an "either/or" to a "both/and" stance. This openness dissolves unhelpful struggle, leading to clarity and compassion. Though grief remains, you'll come to understand that, just as with happiness, pain is also impermanent.

When you stop trying to change the unchangeable, you can take care of what can be change. Everything else you can meet with mindful acceptance. Acceptance is a loaded word; when used unskillfully it makes us feel unseen, unheard, and demoralized. If you have ever been told to "buck up" or "get over it," you know how quickly it can shut you down.

MINDFUL ACCEPTANCE

When the unthinkable happens, mindful acceptance invites you to honor yourself and your experience with dignity and kindness. Rather than turn your back on your own suffering, you treat yourself as you would a beloved friend. You take the time to pay attention to the physical sensations, thoughts, and feelings that accompany your pain.

This kind of acceptance means that you choose thoughtfully how to respond, and temper your response with compassion. You will know you do not need to numb your pain or run from reality, nor do you need to punish yourself through blame, guilt, self-loathing, or feel a sense of unworthiness. You can find the middle ground of equanimity.

THE TEACHINGS OF THE BUDDHA

The practice of mindfulness is now popular in mainstream culture, but the historical context is often overlooked. It may be helpful to understand where these practices came from. While mindfulness and meditation existed prior to the historical Buddha, it's his teachings that introduced these techniques to those of us who were not on a committed spiritual journey.

The Buddha was born Prince Siddhartha Gautama, the heir to a small kingdom in the foothills of the Himalayas. A sage predicted that the young prince would grow up to be either a great ruler or a great spiritual teacher. His father, the king, wanted Siddhartha to be a great ruler like himself, and took extreme measures to surround his son with all the luxuries money could buy so that he would not want to leave the palace.

When Siddhartha was of age, he married a beautiful princess, and together they had a son. However, when Siddhartha reached the age of 29, something inside him became restless. For the first time in his very privileged and sheltered life, he left the royal compound. In that fateful first visit to town he witnessed suffering for the first time:

- First he saw an old man
- Then a sick man
- Lastly a corpse.

Surprised, the young prince asked his chariot-driver: "Who becomes afflicted like these people?" The chariot-driver, Channa, replied, "Everyone."

Siddhartha left the palace a second time, and encountered a wandering ascetic, a spiritual man. The prince asked his chariot-driver: "Who is that?" Channa explained, "That is a man seeking truth and liberation; he has left worldly things behind."

Prince Siddhartha was so inspired that he left his wife and child in the care of his family and became a wandering ascetic himself. He meditated, practiced yoga, and ate very little for six years. Homeless, sick, and nearly starving to death, Siddhartha realized that a life of renunciation was not getting him anywhere closer to the truth.

At this realization, he accepted a mixture of milk, rice flour, and honey in a golden bowl from a young maiden. This act of self-indulgence angered the five ascetics with whom he was traveling. Untouched by their disdain and recognizing the golden bowl as a sign of impending Buddhahood (as it was well known at the time that all previous Buddhas had eaten from a golden bowl), Siddhartha sat down under the Tree of Enlightenment, the Bodhi Tree. He vowed not to stop meditating until he reached perfect enlightenment—*Nirvana*.

As dusk fell, the great demon Devaputra Mara appeared and conjured up many visions to distract Siddhartha from his aim. However, none of his tactics worked and, enraged, the demon finally demanded: "Who are you to seek enlightenment? Who will testify that you are worthy of perfect enlightenment?"

Siddhartha reached down with one finger and touched the earth. "The earth is my witness," he said. The story goes that the world shook with such vigor that Mara and his demon army fled in fear. Able to calm his own internal demons and steady his mind, Siddhartha finally achieved enlightenment and became the Buddha, the "awakened one."

After his enlightenment, the Buddha could see that all people wanted to be happy, but most did not know the way. He could see that everyone had Buddha Nature inside, but most did not realize it. Overcome with compassion, he decided to share what he had learned with the world, and spent the rest of his life teaching what is known as *dharma*, or truth.

THE FOUR NOBLE TRUTHS
AND THE END OF SUFFERING

The Buddha's first lesson is known as the Four Noble Truths. It details the causes of suffering and gives instructions for ending suffering.

The First Noble Truth acknowledges that pain, or *dukkha*, exists. We will all be disappointed, experience loss, and be unsatisfied at some point in our lives, no matter how hard we try to avoid it. In short, we will encounter pain just as we encounter pleasure. Pain in this context refers to an inevitable and uncontrollable event, such as the death of a loved one or an illness.

The Second Noble Truth says that suffering exists because of our attachment to cravings, aversions, and a false sense of security. Suffering in this context is our reaction to pain, which is often unskillful. We hold on tightly to sensory pleasures, opinions, rituals, and the belief that everything is permanent, when in reality everything is fluid.

The Third Noble Truth gives us the good news: we can end our suffering and achieve a state of peace in which we will be untouched by the forces of greed, hatred, and delusion; the root causes of suffering.

The Fourth Noble Truth tells us that the way to end our suffering is through the Noble Eightfold Path. This involves living our life with right understanding, right thought, right speech, right action, right livelihood, right effort, right mindfulness, and right concentration. The lesson is that neither self-indulgence nor self-denial will lead to peace, and it is called the Middle Path.

CHARTING YOUR OWN
MIDDLE PATH THROUGH GRIEF

The Middle Path and the Four Noble Truths can help you navigate your grief in the modern age. When a loved one dies, you come face to face with the First Noble Truth: pain exists. You realize how temporary life is and recognize that at any moment everything you "know" to be true can suddenly fall apart. It feels as though there is no ground beneath your feet. Some of us become preoccupied with our loss, while others try to avoid thinking about it altogether by numbing our pain with food, drugs, or alcohol. This is the Second Noble Truth in action: suffering comes from clinging and aversion, or obsession and avoidance.

The Third Noble Truth promises the end of suffering, which gives us hope in the face of great pain. This leads us to the practices offered in the Fourth Noble Truth. It is often said that if you follow just one of the practices suggested in the Noble Eightfold Path, the other seven will naturally show up in your life. In this book we will focus on mindfulness.

Even in the absence of grief, the practice of mindfulness may seem daunting. If you have ever picked up a magazine with a meditating model smiling with bliss on a beach, you will know what I mean. However, the truth is that a moment of mindful peace is not as far away as you might think, and just that one moment can imbue your whole being with hope. I see this happen regularly in grief groups, and all it takes is focused attention on your breath and your body.

Mindfulness lets you expand your view by placing you in the middle ground between denying your pain and overindulging in your suffering. From that vantage point you can observe the whole experience with a sense of openness to whatever arises. You stay in contact with the entire scope of your existence, and you experience grief without becoming grief itself.

The first step to practicing mindfulness is to understand that there is no right way to grieve. You may have been told that you will grieve in stages, but contemporary grief research shows that there is no single "right way" to grieve. The fact is that each of us experiences grief in our own way. Your reaction to loss is determined by a combination of factors:

- The nature of your relationship with the person who died
- The way they died
- Your physical health
- Your life circumstances
- Learned coping strategies
- Your age
- Available social and economic support (or lack thereof).

Most people experience uncomfortable physical sensations, emotions, thoughts, and changed behavior, but no two people are identical. You may find that relationships increase in intimacy or dissolve completely. Religious or spiritual practice will either provide you with comfort or seem inadequate as you try to make sense of the loss. No matter what happens, if you learn to be mindful of your experience you can learn to respond rather than react.

Mindfully relating to your grief means being fully aware of your experience of loss while simultaneously embracing whatever arises in you with compassion and loving-kindness. This does not mean that you have to be happy despite your loss. It means that instead of fighting a losing battle against something you cannot change, you observe the situation in order to develop wisdom and reduce your suffering.

The Chinese symbol for mindfulness is a combination of the symbols for "now" and "heart." This sums it up perfectly: mindfulness is the practice of opening your heart to what is happening right now. Openness is compassionate and caring: holding the moment in a tender embrace rather than attacking it with hatred and violence.

I like the notion of "calm abiding." One of my meditation friends loves the expression "to be with" what is happening. Mindfulness teaches us that we don't have to fix, label, or judge what arises. In fact, most of the time trying to fix the situation is useless. Instead, we learn how to respond to a situation without reacting; this gives us an amazing amount of freedom, and helps us to get unstuck.

We are born mindful and curious, but as we grow we are influenced by others and by our own experiences. Everything, from how we potty-train to what type of food we like, is labeled "good" or "bad." We stop noticing things "just as they are," and instead we begin to make snap judgments on autopilot. In this way we learn to chase after pleasure and push everything else away. We create a story about "how things are supposed to be." We tell ourselves why we deserve or don't deserve whatever is happening to us, when so often what is happening isn't personal at all. Unfortunately, most of us become cut off from our true nature, deny reality, and never feel that we are quite fully alive.

The death of a loved one moves the autopilot switch to "off." This is a wakeup call—a bell of awareness—an opportunity to intentionally change course. At first you may feel numb. This is normal. It is the body's graceful way of helping you cope in the early days of loss. Eventually you will realize that you need to reroute, but you may not be sure where to begin; this is where mindfulness can help. If you think of your life as a journey, the present moment is the "You Are Here" marker on the map. No matter how disoriented you feel, your mindfulness practice will help bring you back to the safe harbor of the present moment using the tools you already have: your breath and your body. You can then make the choice to leave the autopilot switch set to "off," and instead chart your own course.

HOW TO BEGIN YOUR MINDFULNESS PRACTICE

Mindfulness is both a state of mind and a type of meditation practice. Both are rooted in the idea that the closer we are to the truth, the more liberated we will become. Remembering our own true nature is especially difficult after a significant loss. Nothing feels right. We are uncomfortable in our own skin. You may even be asking yourself, "How on earth am I going to make it?"

The answer is that we are going to take baby steps. Some days they will be really tiny baby steps, where just walking across the room to sit on your meditation cushion is like climbing Mount Everest barefoot with a monkey on your back. Other days you will surprise yourself with a baby leap as you find peace in the rhythm of your own breath for a few precious moments. Eventually you will wake up one morning and realize that you slept through the night for the first time, or you will eat a meal and find yourself enjoying the taste of the food.

Remember: it does not matter if you were naturally calm and healthy before your loss, or if you were always on the go and never thought twice about relaxation. We are going to start from where you are now, and consider the possibility that one day you will look over your shoulder to where you have come from and discover that the accumulation of baby steps (and baby leaps) has delivered you safely to the other side of the canyon of grief.

WHAT TO EXPECT FROM YOUR PRACTICE

The first time you reconnect with your body you may feel as though you are meeting a long-lost friend. The reconnection may be bittersweet, but as you learn to pay attention to the present moment you will move beyond the story of who you think you are, and open yourself to *satya*, or truth. Yes, you feel devastated, lost, vulnerable, and confused, but you are still intact. The truth is that you are not destroyed.

This book isn't going to tell you how to use mindfulness to "get over" your grief. That is because grief-work isn't about getting over anything. It is about learning how to adapt to your life after loss, and finding a new way to relate to your loved one even though they are no longer physically present. I am not going to tell you how to "fix" yourself, because nothing is actually wrong with you. For now, if you find you are chastising yourself for your thoughts, feelings, and actions, and believing that you should be over this already, remind yourself that you are human, and that your pain is an artifact of love.

TWO TYPES OF MINDFULNESS PRACTICE: FORMAL AND INFORMAL

The most recognized mindfulness practice is seated meditation. This can be done seated on a special cushion on the floor (known as *zafu* or *gomden*), but a stack of blankets works fine, too, or you can practice in a straight-backed chair.

Seated meditation is categorized as a formal mindfulness technique because you intentionally dedicate time to practice. Formal mindfulness is like weight lifting, fortifying your "mindfulness muscles" so that when a stressful situation strikes, your mind and body are equipped to regain equilibrium. As regular gym sessions enhance your physical fitness, sitting on your meditation cushion regularly enhances your capacity to remain tranquil amid chaos.

Another formal technique is walking meditation, which can be especially beneficial if you feel overwhelmed or restless. This practice engages your body and mind simultaneously, anchoring your awareness in the present moment as you notice each step. Just as in seated meditation, this too strengthens your mindfulness muscles, helping you maintain calm and focus even when life becomes turbulent.

SPONTANEOUS AWARENESS: INFORMAL MINDFULNESS PRACTICE

You can also apply the mindfulness skills that you build in formal practice in an informal way throughout your day. This doesn't mean that you have to plunk your cushion down in the middle of the mall, of course. Informal practice is an internal and spontaneous act, such as silently sending loving-kindness to people on a crowded bus, or paying attention to the sensations of your body while queuing.

I had one student choose the longest checkout line in order to practice mindfulness of the sensation of patience after a particularly hectic day. "I didn't really need to be anywhere at any specific time, but I always rush, rush, rush. This time I just watched my breath and my body, and recognized that I was telling myself that I would be in line forever," she said. "I found that once I stopped the narrative and became mindful of the moment, it was nice just to stand in line. For that moment, that was all I had to do."

How often do we tell ourselves how busy we are? Every moment is an opportunity to wake up to the truth, no matter where you are or what you are doing. You can practice in the middle of a crowded room and no one will be any the wiser. Try one of these informal mindfulness techniques next time you realize you are rushing around or daydreaming:

- Pay attention to the sensation of your legs while in line at the grocery checkout.
- Smile at a stranger and send them a silent message of loving-kindness.
- Feel the sensation of your scalp while shampooing your hair.
- Pause to notice your breath for two rounds of inhalations and exhalations while at your desk or in traffic.
- Give yourself permission to do one thing at a time mindfully, and let go of the idea of multi-tasking.

PREPARING FOR YOUR PRACTICE

Mindfulness is called a "practice" because it doesn't have to be perfect. Isn't that a relief? Just try to do your best with each exercise, and always make modifications that help you to be more present.

Before you begin the practice below, set aside time to address the basic "housekeeping" tasks that will let you create a foundation for your mindfulness practice. Here are some suggestions:

- **Create your space.** You will need a quiet and safe place where you will not be disturbed. If possible, choose an area of your house that is quiet and clutter-free. Having a dedicated practice space will make it easier for you to show up regularly.
- **Gather props that will support you in your practice:**
  - A straight-backed chair
  - A meditation cushion or firm, folded blankets
  - Two or three extra blankets for warmth and support
  - A timekeeping device: kitchen timers can be handy, and there are a few smartphone apps that serve as meditation timers
  - A journal or writing pad
  - A pen or pencil, plus crayons or colored pencils.
- **Schedule time to practice.** Starting a self-care routine can be challenging. Begin simply with a manageable five-minute daily practice, gradually increasing to at least 20 minutes. Consistency is key; daily small sessions are more beneficial than a single lengthy weekly one.
- **Silence phones and electronics.** If you are used to being "plugged in" during your waking hours, experiment with turning your phone off during your practice. If you do choose to use your cell phone as a timekeeper, consider setting it to airplane or "do not disturb" mode.
- **Dress comfortably.** If possible, wear loose, comfortable clothes. I suggest dressing in layers, as your body will probably cool off as it relaxes.

A FEW NOTES BEFORE YOU BEGIN

There are no "bad" meditators.

There are only people who meditate, and people who do not. There was a time in your life when you did not know how to speak or walk or ride a bike, but you learned. All it took was wise instruction and practice.

You do not need to get rid of your thoughts.

Meditation practice empowers you to manage the attention and attitude you have toward your thoughts, which is far more skillful than fighting against our brain's prime directive to think.

You may get very sleepy during meditation.

Many of us have trouble sleeping when we are in the throes of grief. Although the point of mindfulness meditation is to "wake-up" to the world around you, if your body is so tired that you need to sleep, by all means sleep.

There are ways to work with difficult emotions.

If facing a difficult emotion is causing you more suffering than relief, focusing practices, such as Coming to Your Six Senses (page 29) or the Relaxation Response (page 40), can give you a safe place to rest your mind. When you are ready to tend to your difficult emotions with care, try an investigative practice such as RAIN (page 73). Remember always to practice self-compassion, knowing it is okay to end the practice if that will be most helpful.

You do not have to cry to grieve.

Drs. Kenneth Doka and Terry Martin explain in their book, *Grieving Beyond Gender* (2010), that there is a continuum of reactions to grief. At one end are the "intuitive grievers," who experience the loss on a deep emotional level and will express grief through tears and sharing the story of their loss. At the other end are "instrumental grievers," who will focus on the cognitive aspects of loss and engage in problem-solving activities, and who may not disclose their feelings. We all lie somewhere along the continuum, and experience grief as a blend of the two styles with a primary tendency toward one or the other.

Be mindful of meditation when trauma is present.

Mindfulness meditation can have great benefits for people with trauma symptoms. In his book, *Trauma-Sensitive Mindfulness* (2018), Dr. David A. Treleavan explains that "the three components of self-regulation—attention regulation, body awareness, and emotional regulation—and dual awareness and exposure all help increase our capacity to integrate trauma." But he also explains that over-attending to traumatic stimuli can be too much. If you experience intrusive images, auditory hallucinations, or other trauma symptoms, it is wise to work with a skilled trauma therapist or trauma-sensitive mindfulness instructor when you are learning how to meditate.

MINDFULNESS MEDITATION

The most common mindfulness practice is seated meditation, which can be done on a cushion, in a chair, or lying down if you have chronic pain exacerbated by sitting. Choose a posture that is supportive and at the same time relaxed, knowing that comfort and discomfort will come and go from time to time.

Mindful attention may boost your awareness of tension in your body, which may then release naturally as a result of observation. But if it persists and is too distracting, you do not need to struggle or suffer. If you decide you need to shift your position, simply use it as an opportunity to move mindfully. Remember that you can choose to respond rather than react, and perhaps learn a little about yourself in the process.

PREPARING FOR MINDFULNESS MEDITATION

It may help to remember these four stages when you sit down to practice:

1   Establish your posture.
2   Set your aspiration.
3   Meditate.
4   Close your practice mindfully.

ESTABLISH YOUR POSTURE

Sitting on the floor

Traditionally, practitioners sit cross-legged on the floor on a meditation cushion, but a stack of firm, folded blankets works just as well. There are seven points of contact that will help you to create a stable but relaxed sitting posture. Rather than taking a contrived, rigid seat, imagine that you can sit with relaxed dignity.

1   **Legs:** You can either cross your legs in front of you at or just above your ankles, or shift one leg in front of the other so that they remain uncrossed. Your knees

should rest on the floor and your hips should always be above your knees so that your lower spine can retain its natural curve. If your hips feel tight and your knees don't reach the floor, place a rolled-up blanket or towel beneath each knee. Adjust the height of your "seat" until you feel supported.

2   **Arms:** Let your arms rest naturally on your thighs, palms up.

3   **Back:** Tilt your pelvis forward slightly and elongate your spine. Allow the natural curve in your lower back to support your body. Do not lean forward or backward, but find the middle ground. It may help to imagine pressing your sitz bones into the cushion while reaching the crown of your head to the sky without straining.

4   **Eyes:** Soften your eyelids until they close. If you choose to keep your eyes open during practice, let your gaze be soft and choose a spot on the ground about six feet in front of you on which to focus.

5   **Jaw and teeth:** Relax your jaw and leave space between your upper and lower teeth. Your lips should be parted just enough to slip in a grain of rice.

6   **Tongue:** Rest your tongue gently behind the top front row of your teeth.

7   **Head and shoulders:** Tuck your chin slightly so that your head feels level. Imagine that your shoulders could soften and drop away from your ears. If you have a tendency to hunch forward, raise the "heart center" of your chest very slightly.

TIP: *Most meditation groups or sanghas will have both chairs and cushions available, but if you plan to attend one, you may want to check ahead of time to see if you need to bring any props.*

Sitting in a chair

If you find sitting on the floor leads to a constant battle with your body, give yourself a break and sit in a chair. Most of us are not accustomed to sitting in lotus position, but this should not be a hindrance to your practice. If you choose a chair, try to avoid leaning back against the backrest, and instead mindfully hold yourself upright.

1   **Legs:** Let your feet be flat on the floor and your knees bent at right angles. If your feet don't reach the floor, place a blanket beneath them for support.

2   Follow steps 2 to 7 from page 25.

TIP: *If you feel that you are about to fall asleep, stand up mindfully and gaze at a point on the floor about six feet in front of you, or hold onto your inhalation slightly longer than would seem natural before you exhale, until your mind feels clearer.*

SET YOUR ASPIRATION FOR PRACTICE

Setting an aspiration for your meditation practice will help you to stay motivated and focused. Aspiration is different from expectation or desire. It is more spacious, and not tied to a specific outcome. Some examples are:

• May this practice bring me closer to the truth.
• May this practice help me and all beings to be happy and free from harm.
• May this practice open my heart so that I may meet all beings with an attitude of loving-kindness.
• May this practice bring stillness to my mind and body.

If you set an aspiration and your mind is still full of rambling thoughts, recognize that you succeeded in practicing Right Thought simply by setting your intention—a victory in itself.

CLOSING YOUR PRACTICE

When your timed sit is complete, see if you can mindfully listen to the timer as it begins, sustains, and fades away before leaving your seat or moving on to the next practice. You may wish to create your own closing ritual that helps you to carry your practice with you even when you leave the cushion. For example:

• Thank yourself, your higher power, or a spiritual figure from your religion.
• Chant the sound of "Ohm" three times to connect with the pulse of the universe.
• Say "Namaste," which means "I honor the divine light in you and me."
• Bring your palms together at your heart as you drop your head slightly in reverence and gratitude for your practice.

LESSON 1 PRACTICE EXERCISES
Mindful Awareness: Equanimity Through the Storm and Beyond

Three-part Breath: 5–20 minutes

Coming To Your Senses: 10–20 minutes

Mindfulness Meditation: Breath Awareness: 5–45 minutes

Mindfulness Journal: 10–30 minutes

THREE-PART BREATH

Suggested time: 5–20 minutes

In this practice your breath is your home base, a safe place to rest your attention. Know, going into this practice, that your mind will wander off from time to time. One moment you will feel your breath, the next you will be remembering, daydreaming, worrying, crying, or dozing off. This is totally normal. When you catch yourself doing anything other than noticing your breath, simply begin again. Pick up where you left off, without judgment.

Lie down on your back somewhere quiet where you will not be disturbed. It is important for this exercise that you begin as comfortable as possible. Place a rolled-up towel, blanket, or pillow beneath your knees to reduce pressure on your lower back. As your body becomes more relaxed, you may begin to feel cool, so cover yourself with a blanket or keep one handy, just in case.

Modification

If you are feeling sleepy, you may choose to sit on a chair or cushion, or stand. There is an increased chance that you will fall asleep when lying down. While the mission of mindfulness is to wake up to your experience, if you are in the acute stage of grief or are having trouble sleeping, rest may be just what your body needs. Choose what will best support your intention for practice.

Instructions

1   **Get comfortable and close your eyes.** If you are lying down, allow your arms to settle by your sides, palms up. If you are seated, place your hands palms up in your lap. Close your eyes.

2   **Set your intention.** Ask yourself: "What do I hope to receive from this breath awareness practice?"

3   **Find your breath.** Discover the place in your body where your breath is most noticeable. It might be your belly, your throat, or your chest.

4   **Observe your breath.** Feel the rise and fall of your breath with each inhalation and exhalation without changing its natural flow. If it is shallow, notice that it is shallow. If you feel tightness in your body when you breathe, notice that too. Right now you do not need to change anything or do anything special with your breath.

5   **Get curious about the sensation of your breath.** Imagine that this is the first time you have ever noticed your breath, and be aware of how each inhalation and exhalation feels. Maintain a sense of childlike curiosity and notice that as you observe your breath, the sensations may change.

6   **Expand your breath in your belly.** Soften your stomach muscles. Let your next inhalation fill up your belly like a balloon. Hold the breath for a moment or two longer than you normally would, and then exhale. For now, let your breath stay in the lower third of your torso (your belly area). Stay engaged and curious. Repeat this at least ten times.

7   **Expand your breath to your midsection.** On your next inhalation, fill your belly with breath as before, and then continue to expand your breath into your midsection, just below your rib cage. Hold your breath for a moment longer than normal, and then exhale. Allow your breath to leave your midsection, and then your belly area. Repeat this at least ten times.

8   **Expand your breath to your chest.** On your next inhalation, fill your whole body with breath. Now you are inhaling in three parts. First into your belly, then your midsection, then your chest. Again, pause a moment before you exhale. Release your breath first from your chest, then from your midsection, and finally from your belly. Repeat this at least ten times.

9   **Let your exhalation fall out of your mouth.** Inhale in three parts, hold your breath for a moment, and then allow your exhalation to spill out of your body with a sigh or any sound that feels natural. Repeat this at least four times.

10 **Observe your organic breath.** Now just let your breath come and go naturally and in its own time. There is no effort on your part now. Witness your breath without judgment, along with all the other sensations of body and mind that come and go. Allow your focus to stay with your breath for as long as you wish.

11 **Mindfully return to your whole body.** When you are ready to complete this practice, shift your awareness to your physical body. Stretch your arms and legs, and roll onto your side if you are lying down. Use your arms to bring yourself slowly and mindfully up to a sitting position.

COMING TO YOUR SIX SENSES

Suggested time: 10–20 minutes

During this meditation you will systematically connect to each of your "Six Doors of the Senses," through which your mind makes contact with the outer world. This is a form of concentration meditation, so let each sense be an anchor to the present while you witness how your mind reacts. This will help you to slow down habitual reactions to external stimuli, and instead realize that you have a choice about how to respond.

You can use this meditation before you begin any mindfulness practice, as a stand-alone exercise, or informally as you go about your normal day.

Three Feeling Tones

During this and all other practices in this book, it may be helpful to use the Three Feeling Tones to label your experience:

- Pleasant
- Unpleasant
- Neutral.

This will also help to slow the cycle of reactivity, which includes craving and aversion, no matter what the circumstances.

Remember as you practice that mindfulness is a combination of awareness of the present and compassion. This means that you don't have to practice in any particular way, so, rather than judge your experience, see if you can merely observe what is happening without trying to figure it out or change it.

Instructions

1　Find a place to sit comfortably.

2　Allow your eyes to gaze softly at a point in front of you.

3　Take a few moments to observe the rise and fall of your breath.

4　Turn your attention to the part of you that is aware—your consciousness.

5　Bring your attention to each of your six senses, one by one, noticing if your experience is pleasant, unpleasant, or neutral.

- Notice your eyes and be mindful of seeing
- Notice your ears and be mindful of hearing
- Notice your nose and be mindful of smelling
- Notice your skin and be mindful of feeling
- Notice your tongue and be mindful of tasting
- Notice your thoughts and be mindful of thinking.

6　Allow the scope of your experience to widen so that you observe all your senses simultaneously.

7　Rest in your conscious awareness while continuing to label your experience as pleasant, unpleasant, or neutral. Remember you do not need to push away unpleasant experiences, or attach to pleasant experiences. Simply let the experience of your six senses come and go naturally.

TIP: *You may also use this practice informally while on a break at work, sitting on your couch, or waiting in a line while shopping. Even a few moments spent observing one of your six senses will help you to approach the rest of your day more mindfully.*

BREATH MEDITATION

Suggested time: 5–45 minutes

There are several ways to practice mindful meditation. In this chapter, you will use your breath as the object of your meditation practice. To whatever extent it is possible, let your focus be on your breath. You may be able to stay in contact with your breath for only one inhalation, and minutes later realize that your mind has wandered off in a daydream. This is not only normal, but also common, and to be expected. Once you become aware that you have drifted off, simply start again without judging yourself. Do this again and again as often as is necessary.

Instructions

The first time you practice, you may want to set aside only five or ten minutes. Eventually, you may decide that you want to sit for 45 minutes or more.

TIP: *This is not always a linear practice, so you may move around from one instruction to another depending on how you feel.*

1   Establish your posture and bring yourself into the present by checking in with the seven points of your body listed on pages 24–25.

2   Set your aspiration.

3   Bring your attention to your belly and chest and see if you can feel the sensation of your breath.

4   Bring your attention to your nostrils and see if you can feel the sensation of your breath.

5   Focus on the rhythm of your natural breath with curiosity and without the need to control anything:

   • Notice the length of your inhalations and exhalations without trying to change them.
   • Feel the places in your body where your breath is most noticeable.
   • Observe the temperature, flow, and texture of your breath.

6   When you find you have lost track of your breath, just start again with the next exhalation.

7   If you feel you have reached a point of concentration, try to open up your awareness to include all your bodily sensations, your thoughts, and your feelings without engaging them and without pushing them away. If you get distracted or "hooked," simply return to your breath and start again.

8   There may be a point when you feel you can drop all techniques and simply be present to what is happening in each moment as it unfolds.

MINDFULNESS JOURNAL

Suggested time: 10–30 minutes

Throughout your journey with this guide, you'll be documenting your experiences in a Mindfulness Journal. This is your safe haven for expressing thoughts and feelings without the fear of judgment.

I encourage you to go old-school with pen and paper, allowing you to write in your practice area without needing to use electronics. As many of us spend significant time on computers, writing with pen and paper may feel more personal and less like work.

At times, you'll be given a starting point, perhaps a question or suggested exercise. As with all exercises in this guide, feel free to take them literally or choose your own approach. You might even decide to write more than once a day or bring your Mindfulness Journal with you wherever you go. You can find additional writing prompts in my guided journal, *From Grief to Peace*, an optional companion to this book that follows the same eight-lesson structure.

What to do if emotions get big while writing

Mindful journaling is one of the most revealing practices I have experienced personally and in my Mindfulness and Grief groups. There may be times when you feel overwhelmed with emotion when writing in your Mindfulness Journal. You have two options: you can continue to write or you can stop.

• If you continue to write, use your breath and six senses to link your awareness to the present moment. Although you may be writing about a memory, or a vision of the future, it is important that you are aware that you are writing about it in the present. Feel the pen in your hand; see the paper. Experience the sensations arising in your body. Observe how it feels to tell your story while simultaneously experiencing profound emotion. Notice the emotion as it rises, passes, and eventually fades away.

- If you choose to stop writing, bring your attention to your breath and your six senses. Remember that you are in the present moment, and always be compassionate to yourself.

Instructions

1   Before you begin writing, pause and notice your breath and body. Be aware of all six senses as you write.

2   Write continuously and keep your pen moving. This will allow you to witness the continuum of your experience. You do not have to write fast— but try to write without stopping.

3   If you do not know what to write, write "I do not know what to write." If you find yourself repeating a sentence or word over and over again, that is fine too. Do not worry about the content of your writing. Insights will develop naturally and without effort.

4   Do not erase, delete, or cross anything out. If you feel the urge to do so, notice that urge and get curious. You may even wish to write about your "inner editor" in your Mindfulness Journal.

5   Keep your journal in a safe place or password-protect the computer file, if you choose to type instead.

6   When you finish writing, notice your breath and your body. Complete the exercise with mindful awareness.

TIP: *Feeling stuck? Use one of these prompts as your first sentence:*
- *The one thing I know to be true in this moment is _____*
- *My body, in this moment, feels _____*
- *My breath is like _____*
- *As I reflect on my experience today, I am aware _____*

LESSON 2
CONSCIOUS
RELAXATION

HOW TO CARE FOR YOUR
GRIEVING BODY

Recognizing the body pattern of grief, we can learn to soften to that tension instead of feeling defeated by the idea that fear and anger are our only alternatives.

STEPHEN LEVINE, *UNATTENDED SORROW*

CALMING THE BODY

The body is a powerful messenger. We are all familiar with the sensation of hunger, which lets us know that we need to eat; of tiredness, which tells us to sleep; and of fear, which tells us whether to run away or engage. We receive these messages when we need to take action. We can also reverse this process, and send our body a message. We can tell our internal system to quiet our nervous body, calm our racing mind, and even restore damaged cells. In this lesson, you'll learn to step back from your thoughts, focus on your body, and effectively control stress. This not only leads to a feeling of tranquility but also empowers you with greater control over your body and mind.

• FRANK'S STORY •

Frank married Lynn when she was just 17 years old, and together they created a happy home with two loving daughters. Frank worked for the president of an automotive service center as service manager and second-in-command. Lynn was a community nurse who worked with under-served populations, such as people with HIV and at-risk youth. She taught her family how to be empathetic and patient with others.

At the age of 57, Lynn died from lung cancer, and Frank lost his soul mate and best friend. From the time she was diagnosed, he knew that he wanted to be present to his experience of grief. "I knew when she was dying that I wanted to experience the whole intensity of her loss in honor of her. In honor of the love I shared with her. In honor of the love she had for me."

Frank went to the two grief-counseling sessions offered by Hospice, and then joined their grief support group. "That was useful and nice, because it was very shortly after she passed away—the first two months all I wanted to do was cry. I wasn't crying every day, but when I needed to I cried deeply to the core of my being."

After the group ended, he decided to make a cross-country trip to the western United States alone. He explored Native American sites, learned about their culture, and meditated. "I can't process through blind faith. I have to seek something out. I have always been like that." He felt calm when he meditated at the ancient sites, and when he returned home he continued the journey by enrolling in my Mindfulness and Grief class, where he learned mindful awareness and conscious relaxation techniques.

UNDERSTANDING CONSCIOUS RELAXATION

Conscious relaxation is quite simple. It involves practicing specific techniques that let your body relax with things just as they are. Unlike zoning out on the couch or having a drink at the bar, conscious relaxation is done with an attitude of mindfulness. While the focus is on allowing your body to relax, soften, and open, there will be times when your inner wisdom appears.

Frank found the Three-Part Breath technique (see page 27) helped him to slow down and make time to process his grief. It put him in touch with his thoughts and feelings. "It made me look inside myself and beyond myself. I listened deeply to what I would call God; to the divine. I heard some voice, some spirit moving me. I have always kind of listened for this, but this practice gave me a way to put it in context, a way to tie it in to the physical world."

The practice of mindful stretching—or yoga—was also helpful for Frank. "It taught me a lot about stretching physically and stretching emotionally, too." As he began to explore the sensations in his body, he recognized that he had a severe pain in his right knee, and tension in his neck and shoulders. He remembered that he loved to swim, and decided to find a pool and dive back in. "Breathe, Meditate, Walk, Swim" was the goal he set for himself.

After a few weeks the tension in his neck and shoulders subsided, but the knee pain remained. He recorded his experience in his Mindful Journal, where he observed that he was using the physical edge of his yoga practice and the pain in his knee to help him to explore the emotional edge of grief.

WORKING AT THE "EDGE"

Physically, the edge is the place in a stretch or yoga posture that is not too much and not too little. You are not bored; neither are you causing yourself harm. Yoga isn't about pushing yourself past your limit, but rather about understanding where your limit is. Then you make a mindful decision to move toward or away from your edge until you find the point that is just right; a place where you can observe the sensation with curiosity and open awareness. A good test to see if you are at your edge is to check your breath. If you are not breathing, you need to back away from the edge until the breath is steady.

The emotional edge is very similar. It is a place where you can observe your experience with a sense of calm abiding and openness. "It is only by accepting what is happening, no matter what it is, that you can then choose where to go from there and how to be with it," explains Michael Lee, founder of Phoenix Rising Yoga Therapy and author of the book *Phoenix Rising Yoga Therapy: A Bridge from Body to Soul* (1997).

In Phoenix Rising Yoga Therapy we use the "edge" in a stretch to explore how the physical experience of the body can be a metaphor for what is happening in life. Once clients have the edge in their field of awareness, they can witness the experience mindfully without getting "hooked" by it or pushing it away. This parallels the Middle Path taught by the Buddha in the Fourth Noble Truth.

The edge can be applied to anything. Think of the last time you overate, drank too much, or yelled at someone. We go "over the edge" when we react rather than respond, or when we push ourselves too far. Our edges can move, too. What might seem "edgy" in one moment may seem entirely benign days, months, or years later. When we learn to hold our edge with compassion, we can relax and witness our experience with ease.

Frank knew he was looking for more than a physical edge. "I was looking for the edge to the grief. Not that I would ever escape the grief, but I wanted to find a way to contain it or see it objectively and live with it." He knew the grief would not go away, but that eventually he would be able to integrate it into his very full life. He knew that some day he would be able to walk up to the edge of his grief and hold it with compassion, without falling over an emotional cliff.

REFLECTING ON THE GRIEVING PROCESS

Frank reflected in his journal: "In my daily life I am centered in my loss but I want to find the edge of this so that I can move through life and find Joy and Happiness. This will happen!"

Three years after her mother's death, Frank and Lynn's youngest daughter is studying to become a nurse, just like her mother. "Lynn put that into her head years ago. She taught her stuff about empathy and nursing and teaching and compassion. Suddenly, a year after Lynn's death, our daughter realized she wants to be a nurse."

Frank has also followed in Lynn's footsteps. He volunteers at one of the schools for at-risk children that his wife supported professionally. "I read books to kindergarteners. I take them out of class and read to them one on one. They are like 'Pick me! Pick me!' I love it." He also volunteers for the Society of St. Vincent de Paul, a Catholic charity that supports people in need.

Since the Mindfulness and Grief class ended, Frank, now 63, has retired, survived prostate cancer and knee replacement surgery, and feels a big part of his life is still ahead of him. He continues to swim, works out at the gym, and practices yoga. He woke up after his knee surgery to find a card signed with healing aspirations by his beloved yoga class. He has also taken up horseback riding; a reminder of the American West and his journey for peace.

He is able to recall the precious moments he shared with his wife, and to recognize the lessons of their love. "The end of her life was so—I don't know if beautiful is the right word, but I still remember the last conversation we had. She looked me in the eye and we held hands and talked about dying. She told me how afraid she was. And I was able to tell her what a great wife and friend and mother she was, and I saw all the courage she had to go through the things she'd gone through. Doing this class allowed me to look at these things and process them."

He shared with me a "stunningly clear insight" he had about their relationship during the class that he recorded in his journal: "We lived inside each other. Her purpose was to teach me compassion and empathy, how to love, how to listen, and patience, peace, and self-nurturing. My purpose was to teach her how to pray, and believe in the goodness of God, to help her on her spiritual journey in this world and prepare her for her next journey."

THE BODY OF GRIEF

Easing the pain of loss is not like treating the symptoms of a common cold; for which the remedy of eating soup and sleeping until it passes can be easily prescribed. Like Frank, you can take steps to help your body feel better while at the same time creating the emotional space to witness your loss.

First, let us explore how grief shows up in the body. For some, grief feels like an out-of-body experience. For others, localized areas hold unpleasant sensations while other areas feel absent or numb. Some common physical reactions include:

- Hollowness in the stomach
- Tightening of the throat, chest, and stomach
- Increased aches and pains
- Sleeplessness or sleepiness
- Oversensitivity to noise
- Shortness of breath and frequent sighing
- Lack of energy
- Muscle weakness
- Dry mouth
- Lack of coordination.

There may be times when you want to tune out these unpleasant feelings, and it is not surprising that many people abuse drugs or alcohol to numb the pain.

Unfortunately, this is a useless coping strategy. Hiding from the pain will not make it go away; it will merely delay the grief until the numbing effect wears off.

Imagine that Frank was given a pill that allowed him to sleep constantly during the first year of his loss; he would awake no better off than the day he went to sleep. In fact, the friends and resources that were available to him early in his loss might not be available, and those closest to him would be further along in their journey.

You will benefit when you experience your grief mindfully and develop a mindful dialogue with it. Then you can choose when to engage with it and know when you need to take a break. It is important to trust your own self-knowledge to know when to seek professional support for certain physical and emotional complaints, as Frank did with his painful knee.

THE RELAXATION RESPONSE

For most of us, the body interprets grief as an intense form of stress and switches on the fight-flight-freeze response we learned about in high-school biology. In order for a species to survive, it has to have a mechanism that allows it to respond to threats by engaging in battle, running away, or attempting to freeze and blend in with the surroundings. This response raises your blood pressure, tenses major muscle groups, and raises the production of stress hormones while suppressing the immune system. In times of trouble it is a useful tool for survival, but when it happens over and over again, it is like never changing the oil in your car. It will cause the system to wear out and break down. In people this can manifest itself as something as simple as a cold, or as a more severe stress-related illness, such as hypertension (high blood pressure).

This stress reaction not only makes us feel bad physically, but also makes it harder for us to cope with our loss and the myriad of life changes that are happening. Unfortunately, most people are not taught how to relax, even though there is more than enough research to support the health benefits of what the cardiologist and pioneer of mind-body medicine, Dr. Herbert Benson, named the "Relaxation Response," which is the antidote to fight-flight-freeze (2010).

In the early 1970s, Dr. Benson researched the link between stress and hypertension at Harvard Medical School. A group of Transcendental Meditation practitioners heard of his research, and asked him to study their blood pressure when they meditated. The meditators had a sense that their blood pressure dropped during practice, but had no way to measure the results on their own. Although Transcendental Meditation was considered to be counterculture, and the mind-body connection was not yet accepted and was considered taboo by the medical community, Dr. Benson reluctantly agreed. He collaborated with Dr. Robert Keith Wallace of the University of California on a surreptitious study into the effects of meditation on stress and health.

Their findings show that during the practice of Transcendental Meditation the meditator's heart rate, metabolic rate, and breathing rate decreased significantly. They also observed that the meditators had relatively low blood pressure. Further research indicated that this is a benefit—or side effect—of regular meditation. Remarkably, their findings describe a response that is the exact opposite of fight-flight-freeze: the antidote to stress.

Dr. Benson was able to reduce the essential components of the Relaxation Response to two steps. The first is to repeat a word, phrase, or action silently to yourself. This could be a prayer, a mantra, a name, or a neutral word such as a color or number. If you are practicing while walking or running, you can say "left, right, left, right" to achieve this effect. The second step is to have a "passive disregard" for any thoughts that arise, and to start over when you do get distracted.

The Relaxation Response technique can be applied to meditation, yoga, and relaxation techniques such as Progressive Muscle Relaxation (described later in this chapter). It has even been proven to work during knitting, running, and gardening. All you have to do is focus, repeat a word, phrase, or action, and relax with whatever happens, and your body will be able to stop the stress reaction, and over time improve your immune system beyond your pre-grief health. In addition to feeling less physical tension, you will find that your emotional state begins to settle down, too.

THE FINE LINE BETWEEN MINDFULNESS AND RELAXATION

It is important to note that mindfulness practices are not *always* relaxing. Sometimes, being present in the moment forces us to face unpleasant realities, but bringing the dark into the light is a step on the path towards healing our pain.

So while mindfulness does not equal relaxation, it invites relaxation. If you are agitated during your practice, remember that you do not need to struggle against agitation; instead, embrace the sensation with curiosity and an awareness of your breath. Explore the edge, and walk along the Middle Path of your experience.

LESSON 2 PRACTICE EXERCISES
Conscious Relaxation: How To Care For Your Grieving Body

Body Scan: 25–40 minutes

Mapping the Body: 10–20 minutes

Conscious Connection: 10–30 minutes

Progressive Muscle Relaxation: 15–20 minutes

Mindfulness Meditation: Breath Awareness 5–45 minutes

Mindfulness Journaling: My Body's Story: 10–30 minutes

BODY SCAN
Suggested time: 25–40 minutes

The intention of this exercise is to help you bring your awareness into the present moment using an object that is always with you: your own body. Imagine that you are taking a tour of your body and that it is a place you are visiting for the first time. Observe it with curiosity, and remember that there is no right or wrong way to experience your body. Do not worry about making anything happen, just be aware of your body right now. If you focus on a part of your body and feel overwhelmed, remember that you can always return your awareness to your breath as a safe harbor. You can then either end the practice or choose to resume.

Instructions

You can do this practice either standing up or lying down. Choosing to stand will prevent you from falling asleep, and increase your awareness of body sensation. If you are prone to dizzy spells, stand near a wall. If you choose to lie down, recognize that you may fall asleep, but sleep may be exactly what you need.

Your eyes can be open or closed. You will begin observing your body at your feet, and work your way up to the crown of your head. Do not worry about figuring out why your body feels the way it does, or what you need to do to fix it.

1   Choose your position—standing, sitting in a chair, or lying down—and close your eyes if you want to. If you choose to keep them open, allow your gaze to be soft and unfocused.

2   Bring your attention to your breath and notice your inhalations and exhalations wherever they are most noticeable. Keep your awareness focused on your breath for several moments until you feel you are tuned in to your experience right here, right now.

3   Set your aspiration for your practice. Remember: as thoughts come up, you can simply label them as "thinking," and then come back to the experience of your body.

4   Bring your attention to each part of your body listed below and, as you do so, consider all the sensations you experience. Label each part using the Three Feeling Tones: Pleasant, Unpleasant, and Neutral. Spend some time focusing on each part—there is no need to rush this practice.

5   Begin with feeling the sensation of your left foot. Include your toes and the space between your toes. Feel the top of your foot, the arch, and the heel. Notice the sensation of your ankle.

6   Move your focus into your left calf muscle, and then your left shin. Feel skin, muscles, and bone.

7   Explore the sensations in your left knee. Feel the front and back of your knee joint.

8   Move your focus into your thigh. Feel the front, back, inner, and outer part of your thigh.

9   Bring your focus to your whole leg, from foot to thigh.

10 Now repeat this on the right side of your body, beginning with your right foot.

11 Next, bring your focus to your pelvis and hips.

12 Feel the sensation in your buttocks.

13 Find your tailbone, and begin to scan up your back, exploring the sensation of your spine and the muscles flanking your spine.

14 Feel your shoulder blades and the space between them.

15 Feel the back of your neck.

16 Shift your attention to the front of your body. Feel your belly and abdomen, and notice your breath moving in and out.

17 Bring your attention to your chest. Continue to notice the sensation of your breath.

18 Next, let your awareness trickle down your left arm to your left hand and fingers. Feel your wrist, forearm, elbow, and the top part of your arm.

19 Bring your focus up to your left shoulder and notice your whole left arm, from shoulder to fingers.

20 Repeat this with your right arm, making sure to take in the arm as a whole.

21 Explore the sensation in your neck, including your throat. Notice whether you can feel your breath moving through your throat.

22 Notice the physical sensation of your jaw, the space between your teeth, and the feeling of your tongue.

23 Sense the space between your eyes and the outer edges of your eyes. Feel the sensation of your forehead. Notice the sensation of your face.

24 Feel your scalp and then your whole head.

25 Take a moment to notice your breath.

26 Feel your whole body from the bottom of your feet to the top of your head. Experience the sensation of your whole body.

27 When you feel you have completed this practice, open your eyes and move your body gently.

MAPPING THE BODY

Suggested time: 10–20 minutes

This exercise allows you to record the feeling tones of your body so that you can get to know it better, and take action that will help it to return to a state of balance. This exercise is best done after the Body Scan and before you practice other relaxation techniques, so you can understand your body's pattern of sensation.

You will need

- An unlined piece of white paper, or your Mindfulness Journal.
- Three different colored pencils or crayons to represent the Feeling Tones: Pleasant, Unpleasant, and Neutral.

Instructions

1 Draw an outline of your body on the paper.

2 Shade in each area of your body with a colored pencil or crayon that corresponds to the Feeling Tone of that part (Pleasant, Unpleasant, or Neutral).
Optional: Write what you notice about the map of your body in your Mindfulness Journal.

3 During the coming week:
- Do something to nurture the parts of you that felt unpleasant.
- Celebrate the parts of your body that felt pleasant.
- Be curious about the parts that felt neutral.

CONSCIOUS CONNECTION

Suggested time: 10–30 minutes

In this organic practice you are going to spend some time creating a conscious connection with your body in any way that feels right. Here are some suggestions:

- Roll around and stretch in any way you like so that you can explore the sensations in your body.
- Use traditional yoga postures if you are familiar with them, but drop all preconceived ideas of how they "should" look.
- Massage the parts of your body that are holding tension.
- Lay your hands on the parts that you feel need extra loving-kindness, such as your heart.

Instructions

1   Lie down on your mat or blanket and close your eyes.

2   Take a few moments to connect with your breath.

3   Recall the sensations that you recorded as pleasant, unpleasant, and neutral in the map of your body. Imagine that you can see your body map superimposed on your own body.

4   First, move and stretch the places that feel unpleasant.

5   Next, move and stretch the places that feel neutral.

6   Finally, move and stretch the places that feel pleasant.

7   Lie on your back, and become aware of your breath and body sensations after moving and stretching.

Optional: Answer these questions in your Mindfulness Journal: What is different in your body after this practice? What is the same?

PROGRESSIVE MUSCLE RELAXATION

Suggested time: 15–20 minutes

Sleep disturbance, loss of energy, and a myriad of physical complaints are common reactions to grief. It is very likely that your body is in distress, which just adds suffering to your suffering. This practice will help you learn how to relax your body, which is also the first step towards calming your mind.

Progressive muscle relaxation invites you to alternate between actively tensing and releasing parts of your body. While not a classical mindfulness practice, it will help your body to release muscle tension. Benefits of progressive muscle relaxation may include:

• Reduced muscle tension
• Decrease in anxiety
• Increased energy
• Lower blood pressure
• Increased sense of well-being.

Take special care of your neck and back during this exercise. Do not overtighten your feet or toes as this may result in cramping. Stay tuned in to your body, and do only what you know is safe for you. Consult your physician if you have any questions or concerns. Your breath is a good safety guide: if you cannot breathe easily, back off until you can.

Instructions

1   Lie in a comfortable position. Place blankets or pillows beneath your knees if your lower back feels tight.

2   Close your eyes and take a few slow, deep breaths. Maintain a connection with your breath throughout the whole practice.

3   Assume a passive attitude toward your thoughts. It is natural for thoughts to happen. When they do, remind yourself that you don't need to engage them right now, and bring your attention back to your body.

4   Tense and release. Tighten each body part listed below for 5–7 seconds, then release and relax it for 20–30 seconds before moving onto the next. Move slowly as you tense your body. Release quickly to avoid sustained tension. Pay attention to the contrasting sensations of tension and release in your body.
   - **Eyes and face.** Squeeze your eyes shut, draw your eyebrows together, wrinkle your nose, and pucker your lips. To release, open your eyes and mouth wide and raise your eyebrows. Close your eyes and mouth again and allow your face to relax.
   - **Neck.** Turn your head as far to the right as feels safe. Release. Turn your head as far to the left as feels safe. Release.
   - **Shoulders.** Bring your shoulders up toward your ears as though you were shrugging. Release.
   - **Shoulder blades and back.** Squeeze your shoulder blades together and arch your back up toward the ceiling. If this feels unsafe, wrap your arms around your body as if to hug yourself. Release.
   - **Right hand and arm.** Clench your right fist. Release.
   - **Right bicep.** Bend your right arm to "make a muscle." Squeeze tightly and then release.

- **Left hand and arm.** Clench your left fist. Release.
- **Left bicep.** Bend your left arm to "make a muscle." Squeeze tightly and then release.
- **Belly.** Contract your stomach muscles. Release.
- **Hips and buttocks.** Squeeze your buttocks together. Release.
- **Right leg and foot.** Point your right toes downward. Release. Pull your right toes up in a flexed position. Release.
- **Left leg and foot.** Point your left toes downward. Release. Pull your left toes up in a flexed position. Release.

5   Relax. If possible, remain on your back for a minimum of five minutes or curl up on your side.

6   If you are doing this practice before bed, you can go straight to sleep. Otherwise, come up to sitting slowly, and take a few breaths before standing.

TIP: *Having trouble sleeping? Try progressive muscle relaxation before bed each night.*

MINDFULNESS MEDITATION: BREATH AWARENESS

Suggested time: 5–45 minutes

Use the instructions from Lesson 1 (page 31) to practice seated mindfulness meditation with breath awareness.

MINDFULNESS JOURNALING: MY BODY'S STORY

Suggested time: 10–30 minutes

Follow the guidelines from Lesson 1 (page 32) to write in your journal. You may either use the guided exercise below, or write your own.

Guided Journal Entry

Imagine that your body had a voice and could tell you its history. What would it want to say? Begin your entry with these words: "I am your body and this is my story. It all started when _____."

LESSON 3
COMPASSION AND FORGIVENESS

TENDING TO WHAT HURTS
WITH CARE

In loving-kindness, our minds are open and expansive—spacious enough to contain all the pleasures and pains of a life fully lived.

SHARON SALZBERG

THE POWER OF COMPASSION

When you learn how to send loving-kindness to yourself and to others, you will find that your own pain becomes more bearable. When you learn to extend forgiveness to yourself and others, you will find that there is space for you to heal. Compassion and forgiveness allow you to open your heart and recognize that we all have one thing in common: the desire to be happy, safe, and free from suffering. This is not about enabling yourself or another person to do harm, but about acknowledging both love and pain mindfully. This lesson's heart-based meditations will help you to tap into the healing power of compassion for all beings, everywhere.

WE ARE ALL CONNECTED

Human beings are interdependent. Biologically, we need one another to survive. Connecting with others is our birthright, and when we live in harmony with one another we feel a sense of peace and calm. People and animals alike suffer devastating physical and emotional consequences when love is withheld, and flourish when love is lavished.

Tenzin Gyatso, the 14th Dalai Lama, writes: "Compassion is the wish for another being to be free from suffering; love is wanting them to have happiness" (2003). This is a familiar aspiration; after all, it is what we want for ourselves and those we love.

Compassion is the whole-hearted acceptance that we are all in the same boat. The Buddhist view of interdependence teaches us that your pain is my pain, just as your joy is my joy. There is wisdom in caring for others, because it is the same as caring for ourselves. It is the same as the Golden Rule in the Christian Tradition, which tells us to do unto others as you would have them do unto you (Luke 6:31).

This can be a two way street. Imagine someone you loved were grieving. Would you make time to sit with them and listen? It is more than likely you have a friend who is willing to do the same for you. Perhaps it is someone who shared the same loss as you, or a trusted spiritual counselor or support group. When you are grieving, it can be beneficial to spend time with others and share your story of loss in a mindful way. Not to relive the pain over and over, but to help you make sense of your loss and learn that you are not alone. While each person's particular story is different, you will begin to recognize yourself in others.

THE MUSTARD SEEDS

Kisa Gotami was the young mother of an infant son who died shortly after he was born. Completely distraught, she took the body of her son into the streets and asked everyone she saw if there was anyone who could bring him back to life. Most people thought she was crazy, but a sage told her that if anyone could bring her son back to life, it would be the Buddha.

When she found the Buddha, she presented him with her son's body, and told him her story. The Buddha listened with compassion, and told her that in order for him to revive the child, she would need to find a home in which no one had died, and bring him back a bowl of mustard seeds from that family.

The hopeful but desperate mother went from door to door, but she was unable to find a home without their own story of loss. The compassion she received and was able to return helped her to feel more at ease with her loss, and to recognize that no one is free from mortality. When she returned without the mustard seeds, the Buddha taught her the path to liberation through the Four Noble Truths, and legend has it that Kisa Gotami became a great *dharma* teacher herself.

SELF-COMPASSION

Compassion invites us to open our heart to everyone who experiences joy and loss, pleasure and pain, hope and despair. This includes ourselves. In her book, *Self-Compassion* (2011), researcher Kristen Neff explains that self-compassion has three core components—self-kindness, common humanity, and mindfulness. Self-kindness simply means treating our self as our own best friend, and being willing to take action to reduce our own pain. Common humanity acknowledges that all humans face grief and loss and vulnerability and failure, and we all long to be free from suffering. Mindfulness is the ability to relate to our experience with a sense of balance or equanimity, a calm and clear mind—even when it feels like the rug has been pulled out from under us.

Unfortunately, all too often we take pity on ourselves rather than extending self-compassion. Some of us are hard on ourselves, expecting unattainable perfection even in the wake of loss. Some of us may experience feelings of guilt, or regret at not spending more time with our loved one, or somehow feel we could have prevented the death. Because this pain feels unbearable, many of us will engage in behavior that brings about temporary satisfaction but causes long-term suffering. This includes drinking, overeating, and lashing out at innocent loved ones. It can have a snowball effect.

Why do so many of us not extend compassion to ourselves? Unfortunately, we feel undeserving, and wander around in "the trance of unworthiness," according to the dharma teacher and author Tara Brach. In her book *Radical Acceptance* (2003), she explains: "Inherent in the trance is the belief that no matter how hard we try, we are always, in some way, falling short."

This feeling of failure can be compounded during grief. Rational thinking and reality-testing don't always solve this problem immediately. Our tendency to blame ourselves may have deep roots in our past. Some people were told as children that they were worthless, and have not resolved that pain. Others have been conditioned to set high standards of achievement and want to do everything "right." Even grief becomes a task to master.

• MARY'S STORY •

Oscar and Mary met in mime class in college and were great friends for five years before they dated. They loved outdoor adventures, such as skiing and flying sailplanes together. One year, Oscar entered the competition for a spot on the World Gliding Team. During his flight, another sailplane struck him and knocked the tail off his glider, killing him instantly. Mary was not at her usual post and did not see the crash, but she heard the radio chatter. Oscar was 51, and they had been married for 18 years.

Mary is a successful businesswoman and, in her words, a "high-achievement self-esteem-oriented person." Like many people, she can be hard on herself. Grief itself was, at first, something else that had to be done perfectly. "I had this business plan. I read all the grief websites. They tell you to make yourself spend time with your friends. You journal. You do yoga. You meditate. You do all those things. I had the list and did them all."

Mary practiced yoga before Oscar's death, and was familiar with the physical practice. She came to the Mindfulness and Grief group to ease the overwhelming physical symptoms of her grief. "I guess if you asked me before he died I would have expected to feel sad and cry, and miss him terribly. But I had no idea how physically demanding the grief process was and the stress of that. When I became a widow, the first two things I said were that I wasn't going to become permanently depressed and that I wasn't going to let it define me. The first thing I achieved. The second thing was unrealistic. It does define you. You can't keep it from defining you."

Learning how to practice self-compassion can help you to accept who you are now, without judgment. Self-compassion allows you to let go of any clichéd images of how you "should" be grieving, and will give you the capacity to simply be.

During her mindfulness meditation practice, Mary found it helpful to use her own mantras to focus her attention, much like the Relaxation Response technique discussed in the last chapter. "My first mantra was 'patience,' because I felt like I just had to let things be for a while. And then I added 'gratitude,' because I felt like I had to become grateful for what I did have with my husband and all the good things that were still in my life. Then 'acceptance' of just how much my life had changed. Then 'forgiveness' just to forgive people for what had happened and to forgive things that happened after his death."

Mary continued to deepen her commitment to her yoga and meditation practice and studied to become a registered yoga teacher. After her yoga teacher-training program, she attended a self-compassion retreat. During the guided meditations, Mary found herself speaking the words and going through the motions. Although her mind felt peaceful, she didn't feel any self-compassion.

This changed during one particular meditation. The guided meditation instructions invited Mary to imagine herself in a peaceful place, awaiting the visit of a good friend. Mary chose the deck of her house, and imagined that one of her dearest friends was on their way. "When they said 'now imagine the person is here,' the door opened, and my husband came through, not my friend. And we talked and he told me it was ok to be there. It was ok to be who I was. And feel the things I felt. And so the problem with the meditation was I was trying to separate myself from him. Send him off to a place where he would be in a little glass jar or something."

Mary found that once she let her husband in to her meditation, and was able to sense his loving-kindness, she was able to have compassion for herself and to feel even more grateful for the time they had together. "Even though something really bad happens, I would go back and do absolutely everything over again. How could I not be grateful for that?"

For many of us, as for Mary, it is easier to practice self-compassion if we imagine ourselves with loving-kindness through the eyes of another. This could be a beloved teacher, a spiritual leader, a loved one, or even a pet. Then we can turn our attention to ourselves, and eventually send compassion to others.

COMPASSION FOR BEREAVED LOVED ONES

We do not grieve in isolation. Often, however, we forget to turn kind attention to those around us who have suffered the loss of the same person. While each family member and friend may react to the loss in their own way, each person in the circle is in need of compassionate loving-kindness. Social support is a key element in helping us to cope with grief and adapt to life after loss. Just as we need exercise, rest, food, and water, we also need the support of others.

As we open our hearts to ourselves, we can also open our hearts to those around us who have experienced the same loss. If we notice that someone in our grief circle is being denied the opportunity to mourn, we can take action and support them as we wish to be supported, even as others refuse to acknowledge their pain.

Disenfranchised grief occurs when a person experiences a loss, but because of social stigmas, cultural norms, or family dynamics is prevented from grieving openly. According to Dr. Kenneth Doka, professor of gerontology at the Graduate School of the College of New Rochelle, NY, and senior consultant to the Hospice Foundation of America, there are three ways in which grief can become disenfranchised (2010):

- Relationships that are not acknowledged because of societal prejudice or the nature of the relationship, as in the case of a paramour, LGBT partner, ex-spouse, or former fiancé(e).
- Grievers such as children, the elderly, people with developmental disabilities, and close friends, whose loss is perceived as minimal or whose emotional capacity is seen as limited.
- Such types of loss as miscarriage or stillbirth, suicide, elective abortion, the death of a pet, and the amputation of body parts have a good chance of becoming disenfranchised for a variety of reasons. Some of these losses are seen as not having a big impact, while others are associated with social taboos or are assigned blame.

These are only a few examples of the type of loss that can be disenfranchised. We can use our mindful awareness of our grief to remember that all members in our circle of grief are in pain. They too are experiencing physical discomfort, as well as emotional and behavioral reactions. We can choose to be gentle with them, too.

COMPASSION FOR THOSE WHO
DON'T KNOW WHAT TO SAY

It's very likely that people will say the wrong thing to you. There is no easy way to provide a list of "what to say to a grieving person," since each of us experiences loss in our own special way. Unskillful platitudes, such as "He's in a better place" or "She wouldn't want you to be sad," are usually spoken by people who either don't know what to say or are uncomfortable with pain. After all, your loss may remind them that they will face the death of a loved one someday too. What do we do when faced with words that sting, even as they are meant to comfort?

If we walk the Middle Path of mindfulness, there are a few options. You do not need to deny that the words are unhelpful, but neither do you need to engage in a war with the person who spoke them. Before you do anything, try to turn your attention to your belly, your heart, and the places in your body that are reacting to the painful words. Then notice your breath, and respond when you are ready.

Mary realized that before her loss she didn't know how it felt to grieve, and this helped her to feel compassion towards those who had no idea what to say. "Most people don't know what it is really like unless they have been there. Most of my family and friends kept trying to cheer me up, which wasn't really what I needed. I needed to let myself grieve and be able to be sad, and I couldn't be sad around any of them because they would get really sad and try to cheer me up. Or they would think I was going to commit suicide or something like that, which was never an option for me." She found it was helpful to spend time with other people who were grieving in the Mindfulness and Grief group, since they had a better idea of what she was going through and did not try to change how she was feeling.

Another way to respond to unskillful words is with honesty, while still being respectful. For example: "I understand that you are trying to comfort me, but my sadness is a result of my love and my loss, and I don't want to pretend I am happy when I'm not. What would be most helpful is if you can allow me to feel exactly what I am feeling, and love me no matter what my mood." You will find your own words.

It is inevitable that the nature of your existing relationships will change. You will develop a new intimacy with some people, as Mary did, and let some other relationships go. "Part of me realized I just had to let go of some of those people because I couldn't help them and they couldn't help me. I had to let go of his family because it was too painful for all of us to try to maintain a relationship." Some families experience the opposite effect and become closer after their loss.

ANGER AND FORGIVENESS

While anger is not a universal reaction, many of us experience it. Anger can come in many forms: anger at ourselves for not doing enough for our loved one who died; anger at our loved one for leaving us behind or for engaging in life-threatening behavior; anger at the doctor, the cigarette company, the funeral home, and the state tax administration.

In *Anger: Buddhist Wisdom for Cooling the Flames* (2001), Thich Nhat Hanh writes: "Mindfulness does not fight anger or despair. Mindfulness is there in order to recognize." He instructs that first we should recognize anger, then embrace it with the awareness and tenderness a mother would show her child. Comfort your anger and then transform it with compassion. He explains that the skillful way to attend to anger is with patience and mindfulness: mindful breathing, mindful walking, embracing our anger, studying our perceptions, and recognizing that the person who caused our anger suffers, too.

When Mary's husband died, she felt no anger toward him, as some people do after this type of accident. "He was participating in a very high-risk sport, and that is a choice. I could have been angry with him for that choice. But it was so much a part of who we were, it was so much a part of him." Oscar died what grief professionals call an "appropriate" death—doing something he loved.

Mary did, however, feel angry with the other pilot, her husband's family, the insurance company, and at times even innocent bystanders. She realized that because she was unable to forgive, her anger was leaking out at inappropriate times. "If I was in the grocery line and the clerk said 'Have a great day,' I would get so angry I couldn't look at him. The small things that happened after Oscar died with his family, problems with the insurance, and the investigation—I had a hard time forgiving all those people. I had a hard time forgiving the grocery store clerk." Mindful awareness of her body helps Mary to recognize and then control her state of mind. "The first step is to recognize 'I am letting this build up. I am feeling anger.' Then I can say 'OK, I am just going to breathe or read poetry or go to a kick-ass power yoga class.'"

Mary has decided that she will feel better if she lets go of her anger towards the other pilot. She practices using Right Speech from the Eightfold Path. "I have been trying not to say 'the pilot who killed him.' It is an important thing for me to stop using that language. At first I was talking about how Oscar was killed and how someone killed him, and now I am trying to say 'They were in an accident and my husband died.' It's really hard—but 'killed' is an anger word. It helps preserve my anger. And so I forced myself to stop using that word. I have really just started to be successful at it this year—three years after his death. I want to make it less violent and more forgiving."

FORGIVENESS FOR THE ONE WHO DIED

Like acceptance, forgiveness is a sticky word. Sometimes we feel so much anger that it seems as though we will never be able to reconcile ourselves to our pain. When someone dies with words of forgiveness left unspoken, or when someone engages in behavior that results in their death, it may seem impossible. However, the person does not need to be physically present for you to forgive them, or for you to ask them for forgiveness.

Forgiveness is something you do for yourself. It is a letting go; a shift in your perspective. It does not mean that you deny your pain, just as you do not choose anger as your identity. You walk the Middle Path. You observe your pain, notice where you feel it in your body, and surround it with your breath and awareness, then be still and patient, and watch.

Forgiveness does not always come quickly. If you are open to the possibility that you can forgive and be forgiven, make it a practice. Remember that practice does not have to be perfect: we just have to try. Just as you begin again and again during your breath meditation, you begin again and again with forgiveness. Eventually you come to realize that unskillful actions from the past need not harm you in the present.

As Mary says, "you have to be able to forgive yourself for going on and allowing yourself to be happy. You have to forgive before you can really be happy again or feel happy. I have to keep reminding myself of that and it is the hardest thing." Mary recognizes that negative emotions are going to show up from time to time, but she knows that she has mindfulness techniques, such as the Metta Prayer of Loving-Kindness, to help her when she needs them. She also takes great comfort in teaching the community yoga class at a local studio, and finds that she doesn't sweat the small stuff as she used to.

LESSON 3 PRACTICE EXERCISES
Compassion and Forgiveness: Tending to What Hurts with Care

Embracing Your Heart with Loving-Kindness: 20–30 minutes

Mindfulness Meditation: Breath Awareness: 5-45 minutes

Forgiveness Meditation: 20-30 minutes

Metta Prayer of Loving-Kindness: 20–45 minutes

Mindfulness Journal: My Heart's Story: 10–30 minutes

EMBRACING YOUR HEART WITH LOVING-KINDNESS
Suggested time: 20–30 minutes

During this practice you will use gentle yoga postures to explore the sensation around your heart center, and then offer loving-kindness to yourself. To prepare, spread a yoga mat or thick blanket in your practice space. You may wish to use a second blanket or a bolster for extra support.

Cat/Cow Pose

1 Come onto your hands and knees. You may wish to place an extra blanket under your knees for cushioning.

2 Exhale and arch your back towards the ceiling while dropping your head and tailbone towards the ground, like a cat arching its back.

3 Inhale, look up to the ceiling, and point your tail to the ceiling, while simultaneously allowing your belly to sag and keeping your arms straight.

4 Repeat this for at least ten rounds of breath, moving with each inhalation and each exhalation.

Child's Pose

1 Let your spine come into a neutral position, remain on your hands and knees.

2 Lower your hips back towards your feet and let your forehead rest on the ground as though you were in an upright fetal position. Your legs may stay together or spread to create space for a soft belly. You may wish to place a rolled-up blanket beneath your torso for extra support. Modification: Curl up on your side in a fetal position.

3 Your arms may reach out in front of you or rest at your sides.

4 Notice your breath and all the sensations in your body.

5 Rest in this position for at least ten rounds of breath.

Savasana

1 Come back up to your hands and knees, and find a gentle way to transition to lying on your back. You may wish to place a rolled-up blanket beneath your knees, to take the pressure off your lower back.

2 Rest your arms in a T position: each arm extended to the side with your palms facing up.

3 Close your eyes.

4 Notice your breath and all the sensations in your body.

5 Rest in this position for at least ten rounds of breath.

Embrace Yourself with Loving-Kindness

1 Pretend that part of your consciousness is gazing down on your body with a kind smile. This part of you loves you unconditionally, and wants only what is best for you. If it is difficult to access this part of you, imagine viewing yourself through the eyes of a beloved person, a teacher, or a spiritual leader.

2 Place your hand over your heart or wrap your arms around yourself as though giving yourself a hug. Feel the sensation of your hand or arms, and experience how it feels to hold yourself with tenderness.

3 Say silently to yourself: "I care about you. I love you." Repeat this as many times as you wish.

4 Notice if there is anything you want to say back to yourself, and speak it silently or out loud.

5 Observe the changing sensations in your body.

6   Stay in this position as long as you wish. When you are ready, roll onto your side and pause for a few breaths before bringing yourself up to a seated position.

MINDFULNESS MEDITATION: BREATH AWARENESS

Suggested time: 5–45 minutes

Use the instructions from Lesson 1 (page 31) to practice seated mindfulness meditation with breath awareness. You may wish to focus on the changing sensations in and around your heart center. When you are finished, you may wish to stay seated and move onto the next practice.

FORGIVENESS MEDITATION

Suggested Time: 20-30 minutes

The forgiveness meditation is practiced in stages. First, you will imagine offering forgiveness, explore any resistance, and finally offer forgiveness to yourself and others. Forgiveness does not always come quickly, and so it is important to practice regularly and to be gentle with yourself during the practice. Know that you do not have to complete the entire meditation for it to start to take effect. Just pretending that you can send forgiveness will be a noble first step.

Preparation for forgiveness practice

1   Find a comfortable seated position and allow your eyes to close.

2   Use the three-part breath and awareness of your body to bring your focus to the present moment.

3   Set an intention for your forgiveness practice. Since this can be a particularly challenging undertaking, it may help to remember that you are practicing forgiveness so that your life, and the lives of those around you, will be more peaceful.

FORGIVENESS FOR HARMING YOURSELF

Remember. Without getting hooked by the story, remember a time when you harmed yourself. Start with something small. You can work towards forgiving yourself for the bigger things.

Feel. Notice the emotions and sensations that show up as you remember: sadness, regret, confusion, shame, guilt. Simultaneously feel your breath in your body. Imagine that you can bring your breath to all of these sensations in your body in order to soften the edge and embrace yourself with loving-kindness.

Imagine. Consider the possibility that you could stop beating yourself up for past harms and extend forgiveness to yourself. Imagine what that would feel like in your body, and how it would impact your life.

Explore. If this practice brings up a powerful edge, or you feel unable to send yourself forgiveness at this time, find your breath and continue to explore these sensations in your body from the perspective of the Middle Path; neither pushing them away nor attaching to them. If imagining sending yourself forgiveness makes your body soften and receptive, move on to the next step.

Offer forgiveness. When you are ready to offer yourself forgiveness, place your hands over your heart and speak these words out loud:

> *I acknowledge I have caused myself harm in the past,*
> *Either intentionally or unintentionally.*
> *Now I am here in the present, ready to forgive.*
> *I release all blame. I choose to forgive myself.*

FORGIVENESS FOR HARMING OTHERS

Remember. Without getting hooked by the story, remember a time when you harmed another. You may choose to ask for forgiveness from the person who died or someone else in your life. Begin with a person that you harmed in a small way, rather than starting with a large transgression.

Feel. Imagine. Explore. Follow these three steps as instructed above substituting another for yourself.

Ask for forgiveness. When you are ready to ask for forgiveness, imagine that the person you harmed is standing in front of you. Place your hands over your heart and speak these words:

> *I acknowledge I have caused you harm in the past,*
> *Either intentionally or unintentionally.*
> *Now I am here in the present, seeking forgiveness.*
> *I ask for your forgiveness. Please forgive me.*

TIP: *As you practice forgiving others, it may be helpful to remember a time you have required forgiveness. Try to view the person as a whole, recognizing that there is more to this person than just this one act. Remember that forgiveness is not about condoning bad behavior, or allowing it to happen again. It may take weeks, months or years, but when you are ready, use this practice to release the suffering attached to the memory so you can find peace in the present.*

FORGIVENESS FOR THOSE WHO HARMED YOU

Remember. Without getting hooked by the story, remember a time when another person harmed you. This may be the person that died, or someone else in your life. Start with someone who harmed you in a small way, rather than choosing the most difficult person to forgive.

Feel. Imagine. Explore. Follow these three steps as instructed above, substituting someone who harmed you in place of yourself.

Ask for forgiveness. When you are ready to ask for forgiveness, imagine the person you harmed were standing in front of you. Place your hands over your heart and speak these words:

> *I acknowledge you have caused me harm in the past,*
> *Either intentionally or unintentionally.*
> *Now I am here in the present, ready to forgive.*
> *I offer you forgiveness. I forgive you.*

When you are finished the Forgiveness Meditation, move on to the next exercise or gently open your eyes and feel the sensations in your body.

METTA PRAYER OF LOVING-KINDNESS

Suggested time: 20–45 minutes

During *metta* practice you will visualize a person and send them a prayer of loving-kindness. You will begin with yourself and radiate well-wishes to all beings everywhere. According to the Buddha, there are eleven benefits for those who practice *metta*:

> *You will sleep well*
> *You will wake with ease*
> *You will enjoy your dreams*
> *People will love you*
> *Celestial beings will love you*
> *Celestial beings will protect you*
> *You will be safe from external dangers*
> *Your face will be radiant*
> *Your mind will be serene*
> *You will be clear and unconfused at the time of your death*
> *You will be reborn in a higher and happier realm.*

Instructions

You can practice *metta* while seated or while walking mindfully. It can also be practiced informally as you pass people on the street or sit in traffic. There are many versions of the loving-kindness prayer; you may use the one below or make one up that works for you. The prayer may be spoken aloud or said silently to yourself, and may be repeated several times for each recipient.

TIP: *It may help to imagine that your whole body is able to smile as you consider each recipient on your list.*

Yourself: Imagine that you can see your own face. Imagine your own kind eyes and gentle smile. As you feel your heart opening up to yourself, send yourself these words:

> *May I be happy.*
> *May I know peace.*
> *May I be free from suffering.*

(If this feels too challenging, picture yourself through the eyes of someone who loves you unconditionally, and imagine that person sending you loving-kindness. You can always choose a pet, for they usually offer a generous amount of unconditional love.)

Benefactor: Next, imagine a beloved teacher, spiritual guide, or person who inspires you. Imagine how it would feel to be in their presence, see their face, and smile, as you send them these words:

> *May you be happy, as I wish to be happy.*
> *May you know peace, as I wish to know peace.*
> *May you be free from suffering, as I wish to be free from suffering.*

Beloved friend: Imagine that you are in the presence of someone close to you—perhaps a dear friend—and feel the sensation of their presence as you repeat the prayer above.

Neutral person: Choose a person who you neither like nor dislike. This may be a person you see regularly but don't know, such as a bank teller or cashier at the grocery store. Picture their face, and maintain the same sense of loving-kindness in your body as you have felt for the previous people. Send this person the loving-kindness feeling and prayer above.

Difficult person: Find a person in your life who is challenging. This does not have to be your worst enemy, and it does not mean that you are excusing acts of wrongdoing. If you cannot send the same sense of loving-kindness toward this person as you did toward your benefactor, choose a different recipient until you find someone to whom you can send loving-kindness with ease. Once you find the right person, imagine their face and cultivate a sense of loving-kindness as you send them the prayer above.

All beings everywhere: The final stage of this practice is to send loving-kindness to all sentient beings. All people, all animals, without limits, all over the world.

> *May we all be happy.*
> *May we all know peace.*
> *May we all be free from suffering.*

Reflection: When you are finished, reflect on the effects of your *metta* practice. Notice how it impacts the rest of your day, and how you interact with those close to you, as well as with strangers.

MINDFULNESS JOURNALING: MY HEART'S STORY

Suggested time: 10–30 minutes

Follow the guidelines from Lesson 1 (page 32) to write in your journal. You may either use the guided exercise below, or write on your own.

Guided Journal Entry

Imagine that your heart had a voice and could tell you its history. What would it want to say? Begin your entry with these words: "I am your heart and this is my story. It all started when _____"

LESSON 4
SKILLFUL COURAGE

THE DANCE OF STRENGTH AND
VULNERABILITY

*Don't turn away. Keep looking at the bandaged
place. That's where the light enters you.*

RUMI (1207–1273)

THE RESILIENCE OF BAMBOO

Skillful courage and bamboo have a lot in common. Courage is the bamboo's root, anchoring you firmly against life's storm. Vulnerability is its flexibility, allowing you to yield and sway in grief's wind. These two qualities are interdependent and inseparable. Grief compels you to oscillate between them. Your vulnerability permits the rich depth of human experience, while your inherent courage stands tall against challenges.

• KIM'S STORY •

When Kim was 36, she was pregnant with her first child and about to begin training as a clinical psychologist. Armed with a Master's degree in thanatology, the study of death, dying, and bereavement, she was eager to continue her education and counsel people who were bereaved.

Kim gave birth to a stillborn baby boy one week before classes were scheduled to begin. She and her husband were devastated. Kim recalls saying, "'I can get through this because I am a thanatologist.' I told myself there was a 'right way to grieve,' even though I would never tell anyone else that. I forced myself to listen to sad music, look at his photo from the hospital, and surround myself with linking objects. I made myself experience the pain." She took the first week of classes off, and then began a preparatory course for therapists. The instructor led a period of mindfulness meditation at the beginning of each class. "Every time I closed my eyes I saw babies," she said. "It was very painful and very hard, so I would open my eyes and just check out."

The instructor was very gentle and validated her experience. He let her know that her discomfort was okay, and invited her to stay present with her breath in the moment. She kept trying, despite the images, while at home she continued, in her words, to "force myself to grieve."

The next semester, Kim took a class on Dialectical Behavioral Therapy (DBT), a therapeutic method that helps people with borderline personality disorder to self-regulate emotion and behavior by practicing skills such as reality testing and mindful awareness. This instructor also began each class with a period of mindfulness meditation.

"Meditating was still difficult, but I persisted in spite of horrific pain," Kim said. "I found out that when I started to engage with the present I could sit with the pain. It wasn't going to go anywhere, but it wasn't going to kill me, either." Eventually the images faded away. "I reached a state where I was thinking about him and not rushing it away or trying to avoid it, and then I would move on to the next thought."

A third mindfulness-based course on Acceptance and Commitment Therapy really helped Kim to deepen her ability to "be with" what had happened. She began to recognize that she was punishing herself by saturating herself with grief. "I was born with a genetic disorder affecting my uterus, and I take medication. I didn't know I was pregnant until 14 weeks in. I wonder what the outcome would have been if I had known sooner and stopped taking the medication. I realized that I was trying to make myself feel the pain to hold onto him, but then I realized that he is going to be with me anyway. Surrounding myself with photos and linking objects wasn't so I could heal myself, it was so I could torture myself."

Kim recognized that she was forcing herself to be strong and take on extra pain as though it were a penance. Once she was able to open her heart to the vulnerability of her loss, she was able to consider her aspirations for the future. "I recognized that I was warring with my thoughts and feeling responsible. Now I am able to accept that what I have is what I have, and be at peace with the chasm between what I wanted and what I have. I can just be able to sit with it and ask myself 'What am I going to do with this life now?' I have the ability to accept that I was in pain and that it hurts, but that I can experience this pain and still do things that are meaningful in my life."

This year Kim had a hysterectomy because of her illness, and she will never be able to have a biological child. "When my son died, I was dealing with so much guilt because of the disease. Because I was able to resolve my feelings about him, I was able to resolve my feelings about having children in general. I felt I had to make it right, by either having another child or holding on to the pain. I had very strong longings and desires. That longing isn't as powerful anymore. I am at peace."

Four years later, Kim's husband still feels a strong longing when he sees a boy the same age as their son would be now. "If he sees pictures of a child it sometimes takes him to a dark place. Because our son's life was so short, we don't get to have any happy memories. We only have the bad ones, but I can allow whatever is there, and I know I don't have to feel guilty about not being sad anymore."

SKILLFUL MEANS

In Buddhism, "skillful means" is the art of adapting mindfulness practices to the context of *your* situation. It means that you do not have to force yourself to practice a particular exercise if it is not going to help you reduce suffering. Instead, you find a method that works. During extreme periods of distress, you may feel overexposed when you practice wide-open mindful awareness. If any mindfulness-based technique increases your suffering, practice self-compassion and either stop, modify, or try a different kind of meditation. It does not mean that you failed; it means that practice is not right for you right now.

In Kim's case, sitting with her eyes closed invited images that added to her distress, and she was unable to connect with the present moment. At first, she chose to open her eyes and disconnect, but eventually she learned to open her eyes when she needed to, and simultaneously use her breath to be present. This removed the disturbing images but still allowed her to experience present-moment awareness. This is an example of skillful means.

THE DUAL PROCESS MODEL

As we grieve mindfully, it is important to recognize that some days we need a break; a chance to renew our internal resources through relaxation and self-compassion, as Kim's story demonstrates. Or we find we need to ask for help from others in spite of a fear of feeling vulnerable or dependent. Once restored, we can dig deep into our own resources and find the strength to help ourselves. Balancing these two—strength and vulnerability—takes what I call "skillful courage," a combination of honesty, wisdom, and skillful means. Moving back and forth between restoring your resources and actively engaging your strength is a normal experience in grief that shows up in contemporary research.

Margaret Stroebe and Henk Schut of Utrecht University in the Netherlands developed the Dual Process Model (DPM) of coping with bereavement (1999). It is not a prescription for how to grieve but rather an observation of how we adapt to loss. The DPM illustrates that a healthy adaptation to grief involves moving back and forth between loss-oriented coping and restoration-oriented coping.

Loss-oriented processes include dealing with the difficult emotions tied to grief, reminiscing, imagining conversations that won't ever happen, and much more. Restoration-oriented processes occur as we reposition ourselves in the landscape of life after loss. We take on new roles, learn new skills, and create a new identity, all of which cultivate inner strength.

EMBRACING YOUR VULNERABILITY

Vulnerability is a by-product of love, not a weakness. Being born human means that we will strive to connect with others, and eventually feel the pain of loss. The only way to protect ourselves is not to care, and what kind of existence would that be? We couldn't survive without loving other people and our beloved pets. If you're reading this book, you know firsthand that none of these are permanent. However, you also know that your life would not be as full without them.

The beauty is that your love does not die. The nature of the relationship changes, and the physical loss of our important people can leave us feeling weak and emotionally exposed. The key is not to feel bad about feeling vulnerable. Instead, embrace your vulnerability as the great teacher it can be.

In nature, fear is not a weakness but a siren that warns us of imminent danger. It, too, is a teacher. Unfortunately, in today's society our fear switch gets turned on all too often, but the more you learn how to control where you place your attention, the less frequently you will find yourself in a state of overwhelm. And when you are ready to lean into your emotions in a kind and caring way, you will transform your vulnerability into a resource for strength.

Many of us are too scared to look closely at our vulnerability. It is as though we feel that if we get too close, we will fall into a bottomless chasm. However, once you shine a light on your vulnerability, you will see that within it is the courage to love, to be open, to be authentic.

Just as you would not feel a strong connection with another person if they were guarded and fearful around you, it is impossible to get to know yourself properly without embracing your own vulnerable places. The first step to achieving this is to recognize where in your body you feel this tender sensation. Then you can approach the experience with curiosity. When you look at your own vulnerability compassionately, as you will in the RAIN meditation later in this chapter, you will be able to establish a deep connection with your true self, which will in turn help you to deepen your connection with others.

CULTIVATING INNER STRENGTH

The first year after your loved one dies will be a year of firsts. The first time you do even small things, such as walk to the mailbox, drive to the store, or have to change a lightbulb, will be experienced through the lens of loss. Bigger events, such as birthdays and anniversaries, can make you go numb or feel devastated. Some days you will feel too vulnerable and raw even to take out the trash.

It is not unusual to feel numb at first. It is your body's way of shielding you from pain while it gathers the resources to carry you through. Grief can definitely feel like an out-of-body experience, but one day you may wake up and realize that you are stronger than you imagined.

When we speak of strength in the context of mindfulness, we are not talking about brute strength or turning into stone, but rather an inner strength that will support you when you feel as though everything is falling apart around you. Sometimes this means having the strength to ask for help from a friend or a professional, or taking a day to yourself to restore your energy, as you will do during your Daylong Retreat (see page 77).

You are already cultivating strength through your mindfulness practices. Your daily meditation is developing your strength to stay with discomfort, and mindful movement and yoga is increasing your physical strength and helping you to gain flexibility. All these practices are strengthening your immune system and steadying your mind. You may also find strength in helping others.

Kim discovered she had the strength to stay present in her meditation practice with whatever was happening without trying to change it. Now she has the strength to mindfully hold the space for others who are grieving. She earned her degree, and now runs a mindfulness-based grief group in a Veterans Health Administration hospital, where most of the participants feel that they need to be strong and "buck up."

The support the participants get from one another lets them know they are not alone and lets them mindfully explore their experience of loss. Kim's experience helps her to relate to her group: "Now when I have clients say 'I can't do this,' I know where they have been. I let them know that I know it is hard, but if they keep doing it, it may change their life."

As you move forward on your grief journey, pay attention to the dance between your vulnerability and your inner strength. You can see this dance in nature. Imagine a sapling caught in a storm; its vulnerability allows it to bend and flex in strong wind, but its strength allows it to stay rooted and continue to grow.

LESSON 4 PRACTICE EXERCISES
Skillful Courage: The Dance of Strength and Vulnerability

RAIN: Mindfulness of Emotion: 10–20 minutes

Walking Meditation: 30–45 minutes

Mindfulness Meditation: Sitting with Dignity 30–45 minutes

Mindful Journaling: Skillful Courage Letters 20–30 minutes

RAIN: MINDFULNESS OF EMOTION
Suggested time: 10–20 minutes

When a difficult emotion arises, the meditation practice with the acronym RAIN gives us a fresh way to turn towards painful emotions. This act of self-compassion is a commitment to care for your own feelings just as they are, rather than to turn away from or overindulge them. This practice can be done "on-the-spot" when a strong feeling arises, or during your formal meditation practice.

When we get hooked by an emotion, we all too often focus on our thoughts about the situation and do not pay attention to what our body is trying to say. In this practice, we focus more on the physical experience of the emotion, which deconditions our habitual response, so we can choose to respond mindfully rather than react mindlessly.

Instructions

1   **RECOGNIZE that you are facing a difficult emotion.** Acknowledge what you are feeling. "What is happening inside me right now?" You may even want to name what you are feeling (fear, sadness, vulnerability, confusion, blame, shame, anger, etc.).

2   **ALLOW the emotion to play out.** Let the experience unfold with a sense of calm abiding, rather than turn away or over-identify with your experience. Knowing that you have a skillful way to turn into the emotion will help you cultivate the courage to be vulnerable during this exercise.

3   **INVESTIGATE your experience with compassion.** Connect to the part of you that is witnessing your emotion, then notice the part of you that is experiencing the emotion. This dual awareness will help you focus more on the felt sense of emotion, rather than the "story" of why you are having the emotion in the first place. As best as you can, explore the physical sensations of your experience:

- Where do you feel the emotion lives in your body?
- What is the size and shape of the emotion?
- Does it have a temperature, a color?
- What is it made of on the outside? The inside?
- Is it static? Pulsing? Moving in any way?

Once you feel you have an understanding of the physical sensation of the emotion, start to scan through the rest of your body. Are there any places you are tensing or tightening that you could release? Check your breath, jaw, shoulders, belly, buttocks, hands, feet. Let go where you can. Let be what you can't. Then return your attention back to the initial area of emotion. What is happening now?

4   **NURTURE yourself with self-compassion and kindness.** Now that you have explored these areas, what do you need? Take some time to offer yourself words of kindness and care, for instance, "May I be free from this suffering," or "I care about this."

This final step was originally taught by meditation teachers as non-identification, which recognizes that we can be liberated from over-identification with the difficult feeling (e.g. "I am my anger"). The alternative of nurture as the last step in the RAIN system has been created by Tara Brach, but she points out that the practice as a whole naturally liberates us from a identity defined by our emotions.

WALKING MEDITATION

Suggested time: 20–45 minutes

Walking meditation is an excellent alternative to your sitting practice, particularly if stillness makes you feel anxious or like you are going to crawl out of your own skin, though it is a wonderful companion to your seated practice, too.

As with any mindfulness practice, the purpose of walking meditation is to cultivate present moment awareness. If you have been meditating with your eyes closed, walking meditation adds the extra element of sight, as you will want to keep your eyes open for safety.

Instructions

1   **Choose where to walk.** This meditation can be practiced indoors or outside. If you choose to walk inside, walk the perimeter of the largest available room, or back and forth between two points. If you practice outside, choose

a circular path or walk between two points. Find a path that you can repeat again and again rather than having a specific destination as your goal.

2 **Begin with a pause.** Find the starting point of your path and close your eyes. Scan your body from the bottom of your feet to the crown of your head, paying attention to your physical sensations.

3 **Set your aspiration.** Remind yourself why you are walking. Take a few full, expansive breaths and then open your eyes.

4 **Walk mindfully.** Take your first step and experience your feet and legs as if walking for the first time. Notice the transition of your weight between your left and right feet. Continue to walk at a pace that allows you to be present to each step. There are several optional techniques you can use to keep yourself present. Try those listed below, or experiment to find what works for you.

- Take one step on your in-breath, and one step on your out-breath.
- Silently say to yourself "left" or "right" with each step you take. Check in from time to time to see if your foot matches your label.
- Describe each step as it is happening with the words "lift," "place," and "lower."

5 **Reflect.**

TIP: *Informal practice can be done on the spot during your day to day activities, no matter where you are. This will help you incorporate mindfulness into your life "off the cushion." Try informal walking meditation at a farmers' market or grocery store. Walk at your regular pace and add the awareness of the Six Doors of the Senses: sight, sound, smell, sensation, taste, and the quality of thoughts.*

MINDFULNESS MEDITATION: SITTING WITH DIGNITY

Suggested time: 30–45 minutes

During this seated meditation practice, you will cultivate strength by sitting as the Buddha sat under the Bodhi Tree—with dignity and determination—even as Mara besieged him. Sitting with dignity will allow you to use the resource of strength in your own posture to be still and present, no matter what.

In Buddhism there are hand gestures called mudras that symbolize a particular state of mind. These are shown in images and statues of the Buddha, and are also used by meditators to lend a particular quality to the practice of meditation. The *bhumisparsha mudra,* offered in this meditation, represents the steadfastness of the Buddha as he touched the earth during his enlightenment. It is informally called the "earth-witness" mudra.

Instructions

1 **Sit.** Establish your sitting posture on your meditation cushion, blankets, or chair. Build your posture with the seven points of contact: legs, arms, back, eyes, jaw and teeth, tongue, and finally head and shoulders. Close your eyes and take several full deep breaths and long slow exhalations.

2 **Set your intention.** Set your aspiration for this practice.

3 **Picture yourself sitting with dignity.** Drop your shoulders away from your ears. Lift your sternum very slightly to open your chest. Allow your neck to be long and straight.

4 **Create the earth-witness mudra.** Reach your right fingertips down along your side to touch the earth. This represents skillful means. Let your left arm rest in your lap with your palm facing up. This represents wisdom.

5 **Meditate.** Sit in mindfulness meditation, and as thoughts and distractions arise, imagine they are like Mara's arrows, which turned to flowers before reaching the Buddha. If this image does not come easily, simply label each thought as "thinking," and label each sound as "hearing."

6 **Reflect.** When you are finished with this practice, find your journal and continue to the next exercise.

MINDFUL JOURNALING: SKILLFUL COURAGE LETTERS

Suggested time: 20–30 minutes

Follow the guidelines from Lesson 1 (page 32) to write in your journal.

Guided Journal Entry

First, imagine that the vulnerable part of you is a small child in need of care, and write it a love letter. Next, write a thank-you letter to your inner strength.

STILLNESS AND GRACE

YOUR DAYLONG RETREAT

UNDERSTANDING THE RETREAT

Your personal daylong retreat will give you the chance to step back from your normal routine and spend some time with yourself. Seated and walking meditation, mindful movement, mindful eating, journaling, and expressive arts will help you to be still and present, and to deepen your connection to yourself and the world around you.

It is amazing how loud a day of silence can be inside your own head. For many of us, there is a choir of voices narrating our every action. Some are in tune while others are far off-key. We don't usually take time to listen to ourselves, especially when we want to escape from emotional pain and negative self-talk. Without realizing it, we pick up the phone, turn on the television, microwave some popcorn, or hop online to escape our own experience.

During your daylong retreat you will go off the grid, so to speak, and spend the day listening to yourself and being your own best friend. You will have the opportunity to slow down and pay attention to your body, your mind, and your emotions. You will have the chance to practice the mindfulness-based exercises you've learned during the previous four lessons for an extended period of time, and to deepen your connection to the present moment and to yourself.

People who have attended daylong grief retreats report that after spending a day in silence they feel more connected to themselves, the world, and those who live in it. You will spend some of the time walking outdoors and mindfully observing nature. This is a powerful way to connect with something bigger than yourself.

While it can be a challenge to unplug from the world for a whole day, it is also very rewarding. You will experience a symphony of thoughts, feelings, and emotions—some of which may have been buried deeply for years yet choose this opportunity to rise to the surface. Some will be pleasant, others unpleasant, and some neutral; but no matter what shows up, the chances are that you will be grateful for the opportunity to communicate with these visitors in a safe and mindful environment.

Throughout the day, remember to meet whatever emotions show up from the perspective of the Middle Path, and bear in mind that you do not have to engage or push any part of your experience away. Also remember to honor your edges and to be compassionate to yourself and your body, above anything else.

A sample retreat schedule is provided on the following pages, but feel free to create your own. If there are specific practices from the previous sections that have resonated with you, don't hesitate to include them. Remember, this is your day.

PREPARING FOR YOUR RETREAT

Choose a day and time. Most people choose to begin their retreat at 9pm on Friday, end their silence at 6pm on Saturday and have a free day on Sunday, but you can set any schedule that works for you.

Choose a private location. Many people choose their home practice space for the retreat. If you can be free of household distractions, this is fine. If you are concerned about being disturbed by others or tempted by routine chores, such as laundry or dishes, find a church, retreat center, friend's house, or yoga studio that can offer you a silent space to practice. Make sure the space has enough room for you to move around comfortably, and if possible find a place where you can walk outside.

Plan to be silent. During the retreat you will maintain social silence, which means that you will not engage in normal conversation, talk on the phone, watch television, or listen to music. You can always break your silence if you need to for safety reasons, of course.

Notify your friends and family. Let the people you talk to often know that you are planning a period of silence, so they won't be concerned. If you have children or pets who need to be cared for, ask for help ahead of time so that you can focus on yourself on the day of the retreat. Taking care of yourself will in turn help you to care for others.

Plan your re-entry. Your retreat may bring things to the surface that feel tender and vulnerable. Plan in advance to enjoy a meal or take a walk with a good friend after the retreat to help you mindfully break your silence and share your experience.

Unplug and turn off. Computers, televisions, and radios should be turned off and silent. If possible, turn off your phone. If you are concerned about the safety of other people, such as young children at school, it may be helpful to enlist a trusted friend or neighbor who will take calls for you during the retreat and promise to notify you in the unlikely event of an emergency. Honor your own edge with this instruction, and make sure your safety always comes first.

If you plan your retreat with another person or group, agree in advance that you will honor one another's sacred space and not interrupt one another's experience with words or gestures. It helps to practice "custody of the eyes," which means not looking at one another directly. Designate one person as the keeper of time, who will use the sound of a bell when it is time to transition to the next practice.

Plan your meals. You will need to eat and stay hydrated during your retreat. Prepare your food in advance, or weave mindful cooking into your retreat experience—in which case, ensure that you have all necessary ingredients on hand. Try to choose foods that are simple, healthy, and easy to digest. In addition to meals, make sure you have plenty of water (tea and juice are optional), as well as some healthy snacks.

Gather collage supplies. Read the instructions for the Aspirational Collage activity several days before the retreat, so that you can gather magazines, copy photographs, and obtain any other art supplies you do not have on hand.

RETREAT SUPPLY CHECKLIST

- Loose, comfortable clothes and jacket
- Walking shoes
- Food and drinks
- Meditation cushion, chair, or blankets
- Yoga mat or blanket
- Extra cushions or pillows for rest period
- Grief journal
- Pen or pencil
- Crayons or colored pencils
- White, unlined piece of paper
- Aspirational collage supplies
- 11 x 17in (A3 size) cardstock or poster board
- Magazines and photographs
- Scissors
- Glue stick.

THE NIGHT BEFORE YOUR RETREAT

It is a good idea to go to bed early the night before your personal retreat, so that you can rise early and feel rested. Before you retire for the evening, review what you have recorded in your journal, then answer the following questions, and write down your response in your journal:

- What major themes stand out to you in your grief process?
- What are your aspirations for your daylong retreat tomorrow?

SAMPLE DAYLONG RETREAT SCHEDULE

MORNING PRACTICE

9–9:10	Three-Part Breath	page 27
9:10–9:30	Body Scan	page 42
9:30–10:15	Mindful Movement Basics and Morning Practice*	page 82
10:15–10:45	Breath Meditation	page 31
10:45–11	Break for Bathroom, Snack, or Mindful Journaling	
11–11:30	Walking Meditation	page 74
11:30–12	Breath Meditation	page 31
12–12:30	Lunch: Mindful Eating*	page 87

AFTERNOON PRACTICE

12:30–1:30	A Mindful Walk in Nature*	page 88
1:30–1:45	Breath Meditation	page 31
1:45–2	Landscape Drawing*	page 90
2:00–2:15	Conscious Connection	page 45
2:15–2:45	Mindful Movement Basics and Afternoon Practice*	page 82
2:45–3	Break for Bathroom, Snack, or Mindful Journaling	
3–4:15	Aspirational Collage*	page 91
4:15–4:45	Seated Meditation with *Metta*	page 63
4:45–5	Mindful Journaling	page 32
5 onward	Re-entry*	page 92

Practices with an asterisk indicate new exercises, and their instructions follow this schedule.

RETREAT EXERCISES

MINDFUL MOVEMENT

This gentle yoga and mindful movement practice is designed to come after the standing body scan. Do not worry about making this exercise "look" like yoga. Instead, follow the instructions as best you can, and improvise or modify the movements to keep yourself safe. Stay connected to each inhalation and exhalation, and remember that your breath is an indicator of how you are relating to your edge in the present moment. If you find you cannot breathe easily, back off from the stretch until you can breathe without effort.

The most important thing is that you stay safe. The goal is not to achieve perfection but to achieve awareness. To get the most out of this practice, move as slowly as possible, paying attention to how you enter, sustain, and leave each exercise.

MINDFUL MOVEMENT BASICS

The following exercises can be used at the beginning of your morning and afternoon mindful movement practice. At the end of the Mindful Movement Basics you will find additional practices for morning and afternoon.

Begin by standing on your yoga mat or blanket with your feet hip-width apart and your arms by your sides. Take a few three-part breaths and let your exhalation fall out of your mouth with a sigh or sound.

NECK CIRCLES

1   Lower your chin towards your chest.

2   Moving as slowly as possible, roll your head to the right until your right ear is over your right shoulder.

3   Allow your left arm to feel heavy and hang down by your left side.

4   Notice your breath and your body, and pause here for a few moments.

5   Exhale and roll your chin back down to your chest.

6   Repeat this exercise by slowly rolling your head to the left until your left ear is over your left shoulder, remembering to let the right arm be heavy and hang down by your right side.

7   Repeat this practice at least five times on each side before bringing your head
     back to its regular position.

SHOULDER ROLLS

1   Roll your shoulders forward, up towards your ears, and down your back
     ten times.

2   Reverse the direction.

3   When you're ready to end this exercise, imagine that your shoulders can
     drop away from your ears and let your arms hang down by your sides.

OPEN ARMS

1   Let your arms hang straight down by your sides with palms facing out and
     away from your body.

2   Keeping your arms straight, slowly raise them out to the sides until you are
     in a T position.

3   Pause here and imagine reaching each arm far away from the other, to create
     as much space as possible between your left and right fingertips.

4   Complete two full inhalations and exhalations as you hold your arms in
     the T position, then continue to raise your arms up overhead until your
     palms meet.

5   Turn your palms away from each other and very slowly begin to lower your
     arms again, reversing the direction from which they came.

6   Repeat this six times. Move as slowly as possible.

STANDING ARM SWINGS

1   Move your feet a little wider than hip-width apart.

2   Bend your knees slightly and point your tailbone towards the floor.

3   Let your arms hang loosely by your sides.

4   Slowly start to move your body in a twisting motion from side to side.

5   Shift your weight from one foot to the other.

6   Imagine that your arms are like empty coat sleeves, wrapping around your body as you twist from side to side.

7   Continue swinging and twisting from side to side, allowing your body to be loose and relaxed.

8   Do this for as long as it feels right, and then come to stillness.

9   Pause here and notice your breath before moving on to the next exercise.

FORWARD FOLD

1   Place your hands on your hips, bend your knees slightly, and fold your body forward as far as you can.

2   If it feels right, release your arms and let them hang down toward the ground like a ragdoll's.

3   Pause here for several moments, then begin to roll up very slowly, moving almost imperceptibly, and bringing your head up last.

4   When you reach a standing position, pause for a few breaths and then repeat the forward fold six times.

GENTLE BACKBEND

1   Stand with your feet hip-width apart.

2   Make your hands into fists and rest them on your lower back on either side of your tailbone.

3   Draw your elbows towards each other.

4   Inhale and lengthen your spine, and begin to press your hips forward as you lean your body into a gentle backbend.

5   Allow your neck to stay elongated, and tuck your chin slightly in towards your chest as you lean back.

6   When you are ready to return to standing, use your abdominal muscles as you exhale to bring yourself back up.

7   Release your arms and notice your breath.

FORWARD LUNGE

1   Place your feet hip-width apart and put your hands on your hips.

2   Take a big step forward with the right leg, feet pointed forward.

3   Keep your back leg as straight as possible, and bend your right knee until your shin is perpendicular to the floor and your right knee is positioned over your right ankle.

4   Distribute your weight evenly between both feet.

5   If it feels right, sweep your arms out to the sides and up overhead.

6   Interlace your fingers and point your index fingers toward the ceiling like a steeple.

7   Stay here for several breaths.

8   When you are ready to release this position, bring your hands to your hips, lean your body forward, and press off your back foot to bring your feet together.

9   Repeat on the left side.

MORNING PRACTICE

Exploring the Body's Feeling Tones

During this part of your practice, you will engage in free-form movement. Drop all preconceived notions of what this "should" look like, and instead let the movement originate inside your body.

First, get curious about the part of your body that feels the most pleasant, and find a way to engage that part mindfully, or otherwise exaggerate the pleasant sensation. You may choose to stretch, relax, or massage this part of you. For example, if your hand feels pleasant you may choose to flex your fingers, twirl your wrists, or massage your fingers and palms with the opposite hand.

Do the same for the part of you that feels most unpleasant. Finally, repeat for the part that feels most neutral, which may be a part of you that you barely notice. When you have addressed all three feeling tones—Pleasant, Unpleasant, and Neutral—move on to the next exercise, Relaxation Pose.

RELAXATION POSE

1   Lie down on your back and use blankets, cushions, or pillows to support your body in a way that will let you be comfortable.

2   Let your arms rest by your sides.

3   Close your eyes and enjoy a few three-part breaths (page 27), letting the exhalation sigh out of your mouth.

4   Briefly scan through your body from the crown of your head to your toes, and invite every part of you to soften and relax.

5   Let go of any technique and simply rest here.

6   When you're ready to move out of relaxation pose, curl up on your side and use your arms to press yourself up to seated before moving on to the next exercise.

AFTERNOON PRACTICE

Imagine that you could create your own yoga posture for each of the four *brahma-viharas*, the heavenly abodes or four qualities that lead to liberation of the heart. Alternatively, pretend you are designing a statue for a beautiful park to represent each of the following:

- **Loving-kindness:** The practice of a gentle and loving friendship for all beings.
- **Compassion:** The non-judgmental recognition that all beings suffer, and the ability to open our heart with tenderness.
- **Sympathetic joy:** The recognition that other people's happiness is connected to our own.
- **Equanimity:** The ability to stay calm and walk the Middle Path no matter what arises.

When you have explored each of the *brahma-viharas*, do the relaxation pose as instructed during the morning practice.

MINDFUL EATING

Suggested for all meals taken during the retreat.

So often we rush through meals, for example eating in our cars while driving and not always selecting the healthiest options. Many of us swallow our food before completely chewing it. Sometimes we hardly even taste what we are putting into our mouths. Eating mindfully invites us to slow down, taste our food, and use the process of eating as a practice to help us become fully present.

Instructions

1   Use your eyes to see your food. Take in the texture and color.

2   Slowly lift your food to your mouth. Feel the motion of your arms you do so.

3   Feel the sensation of your lips parting. Simultaneously inhale to smell the food.

4   As you place it in your mouth, feel the sensation and texture of the food on your lips and tongue.

5   Taste the food as you feel your teeth biting down.

6   Return the food or flatware to your plate slowly, feeling the motion of your arms.

7   Chew your food slowly and mindfully, paying attention to the layers of flavor. Notice whether it tastes pleasant, unpleasant, or neutral.

8   Chew your food completely, and when you are ready, experience the sensation of swallowing.

9   Notice your breath between bites.

A MINDFUL WALK IN NATURE

Suggested time: 60 minutes

Reconnecting with nature can be very healing. The outdoors offers many opportunities to use your senses to slow down and even release repetitive thoughts. Mindfully walking while observing what you feel, hear, see, and smell will help you to get out of your head and back into your body.

As you walk mindfully in nature, recognize the fact that you are part of it. Although grief causes us to collapse in on ourselves and makes our world feel very small, in reality we are all part of something much bigger than our own story. You and I are not alone in our experience of the impermanence of life. From the newly sprouted shrub and the chipmunks stockpiling for winter to the rotting tree, wounded deer, and timeless boulders, the cycle of life is evident everywhere you look in the natural world.

I find walking in the woods particularly useful when I feel overtaken by grief or anger. First, it allows me to release some physical energy, even if I walk at a slow pace. Second, it gets me out of my normal environment, away from distraction, and offers an easy space for me to connect with the present moment. If you do not have easy access to hiking trails or other wooded locations, a beach, desert, or city park will work just as well. You can even practice walking in your own yard.

I have led this exercise many times during the daylong retreats in my own city's beloved Baker Park. There is no shortage of nature available to observe. Children play with their dogs and yell, while elderly people rest on benches. An International Peace Pole offers blessings of peace in three languages to our sister cities, and reminds us that people all around the world have similar aspirations to be free of suffering, just as we do. If it is raining, we still walk. Weather is a great reminder of impermanence in the natural world.

Wherever you choose to practice, make sure that you will be safe and well hydrated, and practice self-care at all times. If you end up in familiar surroundings, approach this walk as though it were your first visit. Maintain your own silence and leave your headphones behind. Remember that if difficult emotions arise, or you become distracted from your sensory experience, you can always come back to your breath and body and begin again.

Instructions

1   **Connect with your breath and body.** Pause at the beginning of your path and consciously become present using your breath and the sensations in your body. Consider softening the muscles around your abdomen.

2   **Set your intention.** Ask yourself: "what are my aspirations for this practice?" Remember that your intention may include peace for all beings, freedom from suffering, or a break from your own oppressive thoughts.

3   **Take one step at a time.** After ten or so breaths, mindfully take your first step. Feel the placement of each foot on the ground. Walk slowly at first, then choose whatever pace allows you to stay present.

4   **Feel your body.** As you walk, scan upwards through your body. Feel your feet, legs, hips, and torso. Feel the sensation of walking. Notice the gentle swing of your arms and the position of your shoulders and their relationship to your whole body. Feel how your neck supports your head as you walk. Allow your face to soften.

5   **Hear.** Once you feel connected to your own physical presence, allow sound to come to you naturally. Recognize that all sound is made up of waves that the brain interprets and then names. Consider the possibility of hearing without labeling what it is you hear.

6   **Look.** Turn your focus to your sense of sight. At first you may notice the big picture: trees, a stream, areas of grass. Next you may begin to take in the details: bark, leaves, branches, moss, a flower petal, a blade of grass, a single weed. Let your sight be expansive.

7 **Smell.** Get curious about the scents in the air. The act of mindfully taking in scent will also reconnect you with your breath if you have lost touch along the way.

8 **Allow.** Continue to walk mindfully: maintain awareness of your breath, of physical sensation, and of sights, smells, and sounds. Allow sensations, thoughts, and feelings to rise and fade away naturally.

9 **Close with gratitude.** When you reach the end of your walk, pause once again and scan through your body from your feet to the top of your head while noticing your breath. Allow your eyes to close, and imagine sending loving-kindness and gratitude to yourself and all living beings in nature.

10 **Reflect on your experience.** Spend at least five minutes writing about your experience in your journal.

LANDSCAPE DRAWING

You will need
- A white, unlined sheet of paper
- Crayons or colored pencils.

Instructions

1 Close your eyes and recall your walk in the woods or in nature. Remember what you saw, heard, smelled, felt, and thought. What stood out for you during your walk?

2 Now bring your attention to your body. Notice what is happening in your body right now. Imagine that you could draw a picture of a landscape that is a metaphor for those sensations and feelings. This picture might have the traditional elements of a landscape, such as sky, land, water, flowers, desert, and trees. Is your body more like the beach or the desert? Is it like the city, the country, or the surface of the moon? Is it warm and sunny, cold and icy, or dark and stormy? You may even wish to indicate if it is day or night.

3 Do not worry about analyzing what you draw. And remember, you don't have to show it to anyone. Let your breath and your awareness of your body keep you connected to the present moment as you mindfully draw.

ASPIRATIONAL COLLAGE

Collage is an easy way to express how you feel without struggling to find the words. In this exercise you will create a vision of how you would like the future to be, while at the same time honoring your loved one who has died. There are intentionally very few instructions for this exercise, because there is no right or wrong way to do it. In the book *The Art of Grief: The Use of Expressive Arts in a Grief Support Group* (2007), J. Earl Rogers suggests that you "let the images select themselves."

Before the daylong retreat, gather magazines, illustrations, and photographs with themes that will help you to tell the story of your loss, while at the same time illustrating your aspirations for the future. If you have photographs of loved ones, you may wish to copy or scan them so that you don't destroy the originals. If you would like to use specific images you may be able to find them on the internet and print them out. You can use words as well as images.

Instructions

1 Sit on the floor or at a table where you will be able to spread out your magazines and art supplies.

2 Close your eyes and connect with your breath.

3 Imagine you could tell your story through images. This is the story of where you have come from and where you are going. This is your story, which honors the past and holds peaceful aspirations for the future while maintaining a mindful connection to where you are right now.

4 When you are ready to create your collage, simply cut out the images, arrange them on your cardstock or poster board, and use your glue stick to adhere them in place.

5 As you create your collage, check in with your breath from time to time and use the Six Doors of the Senses to maintain mindful awareness of the present moment.

RE-ENTRY AND BREAKING YOUR SILENCE

If you are practicing in a group or with another person, sit in a circle and one by one, break your silence by sharing what stood out for you during the retreat. If you are practicing by yourself and are meeting a friend after the retreat, you will be breaking your silence with that person.

If you do not have any plans for after your retreat, there are a number of options, such as phoning a friend or speaking nicely to a stranger. However you choose to re-enter the "normal world," do so gently and mindfully. You may feel tender and vulnerable, but take time to acknowledge the strength and willfulness you demonstrated by simply being quiet and still for a whole day. In fact, before you leave your retreat space you may close by sending some metta to yourself in gratitude.

LESSON 5
GETTING UNSTUCK

OPPORTUNITIES FOR AWAKENING

A further sign of health is that we don't become undone by fear and trembling, but we take it as a message that it's time to stop struggling and look directly at what's threatening us.

PEMA CHÖDRÖN, *THE PLACES THAT SCARE YOU*

NAVIGATING GRIEF'S ROADBLOCKS

Feeling stuck in grief can conjure up a lot of fear, and the fatalistic question: "Will I feel like this forever?" Fortunately the perception and reality of being "stuck" are distinct. Feeling stuck is normal. Grief often progresses more slowly than expected, and when you feel bad, time feels like it stands still. Instead of trying to avoid, rush, or criticize your process, it will be helpful in the long run to learn how to identify and tend to any roadblocks with mindfulness-based remedies, which will create space for personal growth and awakening.

• KATE'S STORY •

When Kate was in college, she discovered the body of her friend after his suicide. She was angry, anxious, and sad, and resorted to self-injury and substance abuse to mask her pain. "I have always been a person with a temper, and have dealt with terrible anxiety since childhood, but the suicide of a close friend increased whatever negative tendencies I had, and rendered all means of coping with stress useless. I became very angry after my friend died; with him for leaving, with myself for not saving him, with his family, with God, with therapists, with medication. You name it, I was angry with it," Kate explains.

Although she did not realize it at the time, Kate cut herself off from other people, afraid that they, too, would leave her. She developed social anxiety and found many ways to numb her pain: "Habits that were normal, even healthy, got blown out of proportion: I exercised even more vigorously, often burning more calories than I had consumed that day and almost fainting; I replaced meals with coffee; I studied my heart out, worked a graveyard shift, and wrote and painted all night long. To avoid my PTSD [Post-Traumatic Stress Disorder] symptoms, I kept myself constantly occupied, or tried to. And if there was a second of time that memories, grief, or loss would overwhelm me, I would injure myself. At this time pain somehow grounded me, made me feel that I was still alive, and I turned to self-inflicted pain again and again."

Fortunately, Kate stopped engaging in self-injury and drinking while she was still in college, and after graduation she forced herself to start over by moving to a new town and getting a new job. She started eating and sleeping regularly, reduced her caffeine intake, and stopped her aggressive workouts. She even joined a weekly mindfulness meditation group at a local holistic center. The group was open to everyone, and was not specifically for grief. At the time, Kate was not looking for grief support, but was seeking relief from a myriad of physical symptoms that the medical community was unable to diagnose. "The problem was that I didn't feel any better, I didn't know how to deal with life without all my vices. I had started to experience physical symptoms: pain, exhaustion, nausea, sadness, disorientation, and confusion. I was tested for everything under the sun, and all 13 blood tests, multiple evaluations, and allergy tests turned up nothing. Really, I didn't select mindfulness to help me deal with the death of my friend; I was just at the end of my rope, with no ideas on how to deal with anything any more."

Kate's mindfulness meditation practice gave her the space to observe her thoughts and feelings with the spaciousness of calm abiding, allowing her to recognize that her grief was mummified. Without her old habits, the pain of grief that she had resisted facing was the same pain that was causing her to feel unsettled and anxious more than four years later. As she learned to open up to present moment awareness, she gained insight into why she always felt unsatisfied and anxious. "Once the basic principles of mindfulness were explained, it didn't take long for me to reestablish a connection with the current moment, and to notice how much time I spent angry and anxious at nothing in particular, it was just the state I was frozen in. I was locked in my own time warp made up of fear, anger, and victimization. With some help I realized that I was always unhappy because I had been waiting to return to the way my life was before my friend committed suicide."

What started out as a last-ditch effort to ease physical suffering turned into a liberating experience for Kate. No longer trapped in a cage of grief, she is able to see her pain through a clear lens of awareness. She is able to accept that she is forever changed, without fighting reality. "Mindfulness has made it possible for me to realize that I cannot have my old life back, that there is no old life, there is only this life, and my life happens to contain the death of a very close friend at a young age. I still get upset with my friend for killing himself and so altering my view of life, for making me so aware of impermanence and pain. I still get sad, and overwhelmed by memories, anxiety, and even anger. But I am learning that those feelings and memories have only as much power as I give them. I can see my memories and emotions for what they are: memories and emotions. They are not me, or not all of me in any case, and I do not want to be overwhelmed by them anymore. After years of being locked in grief and shut to so much experience, this feels like a huge opening up of possibility. At times so much change and possibility and growth seems scary, but then part of me says, 'Now you are afraid of good things?' I cannot point out specific ways that I apply mindfulness, it just feels like another option for each moment, one I didn't know I had before."

Some of us embark on a healing journey through grief immediately after our loved one dies. Some of us, like Kate, come up against a pain so unbearable that we will do anything to avoid facing it. Kate's excessive drinking and self-injury were manifestations of aversion, one of the Five Hindrances to mindfulness practice. While most bereaved people do not engage in self-injury, many of us find some method, at least initially, to turn away from our pain.

Kate now says: "I am inspired in a million tiny ways to deal with myself, my body, my memory, my life, and those around me in a kinder, more accepting way. As I said, I stumble often, but I no longer feel as though I will never recover from the loss of my friend."

It takes skillful courage and determination to train the mind to be steady even at the best of times. That is why having an aspiration for practice is so important. Kate knew her body was telling her that something was not right, and she had the hope that it could be better. This gave her the strength to stay with her vulnerability. We need to know why we are sitting, and to recognize that the reason we are willing to face our pain is to reduce our suffering. Logically we understand this, but the mind is so conditioned to turning away from pain that pitfalls to practice will undoubtedly show up.

THE FIVE MENTAL HINDRANCES

The Buddha described five common distractions that lure us away from present moment awareness. They are not unique to grief, but show up throughout our life, and are experienced on and off the meditation cushion. You may not have all five, but you may find that there is one in particular that shows up more often than the others. They are:

- Sensual desire
- Aversion and ill will
- Sleepiness
- Restlessness and remorse
- Skeptical doubt.

Contemporary grief research shows that suppressing difficult emotions can lead to a complicated grief reaction. This parallels the mindfulness instruction to walk the Middle Path. The most skillful way to address any of the Five Mental Hindrances is to first acknowledge its presence. You can do this by practicing the technique of mental noting, which is simply to call it what it is.

For instance, if you are sitting on your meditation seat and recognize that you are feeling anxious, you may simply say to yourself, without judgment, "I am aware of anxiety." Then get curious and explore how anxiety feels in your body. Where does it show up? What is its size, its shape, its color? You may notice that your mind is racing, your breath shallow, and your legs jumpy, and so you invite your breath to deepen and explore the sensation in your legs with curiosity. Drop whatever story is showing up about why this is happening, and instead connect with the direct experience, and respond with skillful means.

Just as it is unhelpful to beat yourself up for having common grief reactions, it is unhelpful to berate yourself when you encounter a hindrance. Instead of labeling yourself a "bad meditator," which can do no good, recognize the hindrance as an object of mindfulness and use it to deepen your insight. The fact that you were aware enough to notice the distraction means you are in a mindful state. Let's explore each of the Five Mental Hindrances individually. At the end of this chapter, you'll find instructions on how to work with these difficult states of mind, both on and off the meditation cushion.

SENSUAL DESIRE

Sensual desire includes physical cravings that range from hunger to sexual attraction. For most people, the most painful part of loss is the cavern of loneliness inside the heart. At first this may feel never-ending, but then you will suddenly realize that for a second you forgot about your loss, only to have reality come crashing down on top of you once more. You may reach for the phone to make a call before you remember that no one is there to answer. Or you may wake up feeling peaceful after a good night's sleep, and suddenly realize that the bed is empty. These moments can make us feel crazy—and enhance our sense of loneliness.

Loneliness is one of the most difficult feelings to tolerate when you are grieving. You may be able to find social support, but that is very different from replacing the emotional bond you had with your spouse, child, parent, or other person close to you. Sometimes you may sense the presence of your loved one. A small percentage of people experience auditory hallucinations. These experiences are a normal part of grief.

Desire is not considered to be inherently bad. In fact, without it we would not have any motivation to continue as a species. We would not experience compassion and love. In Buddhist terms, there are two kinds of desire: unhealthy and healthy. Greed, jealousy, lust, and attachment to specific results—or expectations—are unhealthy forms of desire. Compassionate aspirations, such as the desire for our family to be safe, for our children to be happy, for there to be peace in the world, and for our minds to be liberated, are examples of healthy desire.

Desire stems from our attachment to people and to pleasurable states of mind, as well as to material possessions. If there is an estate to distribute, greed can rise up and rip families apart. The dispute can be over a sentimental object of little monetary value, such as a favorite piece of jewelry or a photograph. At other times, greed is financial in nature, as in the case of real estate or investments. Just when the grieving family members need one another the most, they pick sides and go to war with one another; this creates even more suffering.

AVERSION AND ILL WILL

Aversion is the tendency to avoid unpleasant states of mind, including anger, hatred, and sadness, the most common feeling experienced after a loss. We might suppress painful emotions through unhealthy methods of coping, such as drinking, over- or under-eating, excessive sleeping, or self-injury, which only compound our suffering. Self-medication, such as excessive drug use, is one of the factors that can contribute to delayed grief, which has its own set of difficulties. When we don't face our pain in tandem with others who have experienced the same loss, we may lose valuable social support, grieving rituals, and bereavement resources.

Sometimes we experience aversion to our own behavior—commonly showing forgetfulness, absent-mindedness, hypersensitivity, and irritability—and sometimes our aversion is toward other people. Instead of ostracizing yourself for these natural reactions, first acknowledge them and then get curious about how they feel in your body. Learn to recognize them, so that you can pause when they arise and choose how to respond.

People may encourage you to avoid difficult emotions by telling you to keep busy. This will not reduce your suffering. Grief is not something that passes with time alone. In fact, research conducted by Dr. Robert Neimeyer, a psychology professor at the University of Memphis and Director of the Portland Institute for Loss and Transition, indicates that it is not the passage of time but what you do with the time that matters (2006). Time contributes to only 1% of your adaptation to grief. So while forcing yourself to grieve is not helpful, as Kim did initially after the loss of her son, neither is avoiding it, as Kate did after her friend died by suicide. As long as Kate dodged her grief, she remained stuck. Her pain did not diminish over time—it camouflaged itself in the form of physical symptoms. Once she began to practice mindfulness meditation, she created the space she needed to heal her body and reduce her suffering.

SLEEPINESS

During the early days of your grief you will most likely experience sleep disturbance and feel fatigued. You might be more tired than usual, wake up in the middle of the night from nightmares and loneliness, or not be able to sleep at all. Sleepiness may just be a sign that you need more rest, and the skillful approach is to take a nap. Before you abandon your meditation practice, though, explore other primary sources of your fatigue.

If you are getting plenty of rest and are eating a balanced diet but still feel sleepy, you may be experiencing the hindrance of sloth and torpor. This is a familiar distraction to those of us who meditate. It appears as dullness in the mind and a sense of being disconnected from our experience. Sometimes it results in an upright, head-bobbing almost-sleep. If your practice is not alert and focused, the rhythm of your breath may entice you to sleep, like your own internal white-noise machine. Sleepiness can also be your mind's way of avoiding difficult emotions, which makes it a side effect of aversion.

RESTLESSNESS AND REMORSE

Restlessness is another common response to grief. The opposite of sleepiness, it is often experienced as a strong physical urge, such as the desire to leave your meditation seat or the feeling that you are going to crawl out of your skin. Mental restlessness manifests itself as worry, insecurity, excessive planning, and an inability to focus the mind. As your brain struggles to make sense of your loss and to adapt to this new situation, you will understandably feel jumpy and distracted.

Guilt and remorse are also included in this hindrance. Although not everyone experiences guilt when a loved one dies, it is a common reaction to loss. In Buddhism, guilt and remorse have two different qualities. Guilt is self-blame coupled with the sense of self-loathing. Remorse, on the other hand, is the genuine acknowledgment of pain you have actually caused, whether intentionally or unintentionally. It is the recognition that although you have caused harm, you cannot go back and change the past. You can, however, learn from it, make amends, and move forward. It can be tended to through the practice of forgiveness and compassion.

When we repeat "I should have …" again and again, we are experiencing guilt. "I should have been nicer when he was alive." "I should have called 911 sooner."

We are restless over something that happened in the past, something we cannot change. For most of us, the guilt we feel after a loved one dies is short-lived. We know we really did not do anything wrong, but our brain is seeking answers to the question "Why?" As it explores the possibilities, we get caught in the crossfire with self-blame. This may feel real, but it is usually not true, and dissipates over time.

If self-loathing continues, or our anger at the person who died turns inward and becomes anger toward ourselves, we risk having a complicated grief experience. Although our feelings of sadness after someone dies are similar to the quality of feelings experienced in clinical depression, the two are not the same. Prolonged feelings of generalized guilt should be addressed with a grief counselor or mental-health professional.

Another common form of restlessness after the death of a loved one is hypervigilance. If you feel that you are constantly scanning the surrounding environment for threats, are overly sensitive to sound, and find that your eyes have a hard time staying shut, you may be experiencing hypervigilance. Particular environmental stimuli, such as the sound of a specific ringtone or the sight of an ambulance, may trigger this reaction.

When the body perceives a threat and is unable to process it or bring closure to the stimulus, the fight-flight-freeze mechanism shifts into overdrive. While this is a natural grief response, particularly for sudden and traumatic losses, it is also a symptom of PTSD. If you are experiencing trauma symptoms, including avoidance, hypervigilance, or reliving the event again and again, it is important to seek out a mental-health professional who can support you and help you to ease your suffering. You should not practice mindfulness meditation without professional support if you are experiencing PTSD.

SKEPTICAL DOUBT: LACK OF COMMITMENT

When I tell people I teach meditation, they usually say: "Oh, I can't do that! My mind won't sit still." This self-doubt prevents many people from even taking a chance on meditation, whether they are grieving or not. We all have the natural ability to be calm; we just need to take the time to learn how. Some people think the payoff is not worth the time it takes to establish a practice. Others are not convinced that mindfulness practice will reduce suffering, and call the benefits themselves into question.

If you are practicing mindfulness already, doubt about whether you are "doing it right" can manifest itself as lack of commitment to your regular sitting practice. Perhaps you are questioning your skills or technique, or think that just reading a book will have the same effect as the actual practice.

Doubt doesn't show up as much as the other four hindrances in my Mindfulness and Grief groups. Most participants tell me their physical and emotional pain is so bad that they are willing to try anything to reduce their suffering, and that they have heard at least anecdotally that meditation can reduce their physical complaints, too. A few are convinced that it will work because of the plethora of scientific literature that supports the benefits of mindfulness, and are willing to invest in their own well-being.

There are times, however, when doubt arises because something unexpected trips us up. Just when we think we are about to win the gold medal at the Mindfulness Olympics and have completely integrated our loss into our life, we encounter a thought, memory, or feeling that takes us back to square one. We rage against reality. We are sad and angry, and scream to ourselves that life isn't fair. Or retreat into isolation, feeling defeated.

This is also normal, but it is critical to recognize that you can keep going, and use your skillful courage to begin again. Doubt is a reminder to stay curious. Put on your imaginary lab coat, observe your experience with calm detachment, and seek wisdom in community, therapy, books, classes, grief groups, and all other resources you have available.

GRATITUDE FOR WHAT REMAINS

Gratitude is a gentle beacon of hope that can move you beyond all roadblocks. It helps you acknowledge and cherish the sources of light still shining within the darker corridors of your pain. The memories, relationships, and moments of joy that continue to exist alongside your loss are all reminders of the beauty that persists in your life. By recognizing and honoring these moments, you begin to expand your perspective and understand that while grief is something you learn to live with, it does not wholly define our existence. Through this practice, we can make space for the coexistence of sorrow and joy, enriching our understanding of life's complex narrative.

While it doesn't minimize the enormity of your loss, it does help you navigate the tumultuous seas of sorrow with a greater sense of balance. The act of acknowledging what you are grateful for creates a counterweight to the heaviness of your grief, fostering a stronger resilience to withstand the waves of loss. This allows you to continue moving forward, not in a denial of grief, but in a profound acceptance of it. By weaving gratitude into your grief journey, as you will learn to do in the exercise below, you build an emotional reservoir that will help you weather the storm, and acknowledge your sorrow while also cherishing the good that remains.

LESSON 5 PRACTICE EXERCISES
Getting Unstuck: Opportunities for Awakening

Walking Meditation: 40 minutes

Mindfulness Meditation: Tending to the Five Mental Hindrances: 45 minutes

Gratitude Visualization: 15 minutes

Mindful Journaling: Transforming Roadblocks into Green Lights: 10–20 minutes

WALKING MEDITATION

Suggested time: 40 minutes

Follow the instructions for walking meditation practice on page 74 before your mindfulness meditation practice. Notice if you get distracted, and if so, investigate that distraction through the lens of the Five Mental Hindrances. Notice what arises, embrace it with compassion, and then bring your focus back.

MINDFULNESS MEDITATION: TENDING TO THE FIVE MENTAL HINDRANCES

Suggested time: 45 minutes

We can usually sense a hindrance when we experience resistance in our breath. We hold on to it tightly and don't even realize that we have cut off our own life force. That is why the breath is such a powerful barometer: it can tell us the weather forecast for our internal landscape. Unlike atmospheric weather, we can attend to our breath and soften the inner hailstorm into a gentle rain. When we anchor our attention to our breath, we can get curious about what is pulling us away from our practice or causing us to raise our guard.

Instructions

Sit in mindfulness meditation (page 31). When you notice that you have become distracted, observe which of the five hindrances is present, and follow the steps below:

Mental note: Start with the mental note: "I am aware of _____ [insert hindrance]," and explore how this feels in your body. You can also label your experience, not to accuse it but to acknowledge it: "anger," "fear," "hunger," "sleepiness."

Physical awareness: Notice how your body is responding to the hindrance. Where does it live in your body? Once you have found that place, get curious about its size, shape, and texture, and see if you can notice this part of your body while simultaneously noticing your breath.

Drop the story: Let go of any story that you might be telling yourself about the situation that is distracting you, and instead connect to the direct physical sensation of suffering. Let your breath and your physical body bring you into the present moment.

Address the hindrance: Use any one of the skillful means listed below to engage your primary hindrance, which will help you to gain insight and become unstuck.

Begin again: Once you feel you have softened the reaction caused by the hindrance and are able to stay present without distraction, simply begin your meditation practice again.

TENDING TO AVERSION

Inquiry: Ask yourself: "What lies underneath this feeling of aversion? Fear? Guilt? Aggression? Shame?" What would happen if you could let go of aversion and tend to the actual feeling you are experiencing?

Practice compassion: If your primary aversion is directed toward a person, perhaps even yourself or the person who died, see if you can connect with a sense of compassion as you think of that person. Imagine seeing their face and saying "I forgive you. I love you." If this does not feel accessible right now, simply have compassion for the part of you that is suffering.

Restore your resources as needed: In the early days of grief, aversion is your body's way of protecting you while you restore your resources. If you sense that this is the case, practice skillful courage, and use your breath to anchor yourself in the present moment until you have the strength to sit with the difficult emotions.

TENDING TO DESIRE

Inquiry: Ask yourself: "What lies underneath this feeling of desire? Longing? Greed? Lust? Fear?" Recognize the attachment to wanting things to be different from the way they are, and the struggle that attachment creates.

Practice gratitude: Open your awareness to the things you are grateful for. Start with offering thanks for your breath, your body, even for clean drinking water. Buddhism encourages us to be grateful for "this precious human birth." At the end of your practice, write out a gratitude list.

Noble friendship: After a loved one dies, it is normal to experience a sense of yearning for them, and it is helpful for us to form new bonds as we adapt to our loss. Grief support groups and classes in mindfulness meditation and yoga will give you the social support you need and help to temper your suffering. It may also be helpful to receive bodywork, such as massage or a Phoenix Rising Yoga Therapy session. While none of this can replace your loved one, your body will benefit from nurturing touch.

TENDING TO SLEEPINESS

Inquiry: Ask yourself: "What is the source of my sleepiness? Is my attention as focused as possible? What would happen if I focused on just this moment—just this one breath?"

Aim and sustain: Use the practice of aiming and sustaining. Aim to focus on one thing, and do your best to sustain awareness. When you drift off, simply aim and sustain again.

Open your eyes: Gaze softly at a point on the floor a few feet in front of you. If that doesn't work, stand up.

Sleep as needed: Consider biological reasons, such as poor sleep habits or diet. This can be a sign that you need to take better care of your body. If you believe you are sleepy because you are recently bereaved, you may simply need to sleep. If sleep disturbance continues for an extended period of time or causes you extreme distress, consult a grief counselor or mental-health professional.

TENDING TO RESTLESSNESS

Spacious awareness: Imagine that your awareness is a large container, like a balloon, and simply let your restless thoughts bounce around inside. Rather than trying to control these thoughts, focus on them. Watch them as you would a moth dancing around a flame, without trying to solve any problems or answer any questions. Notice that however painful your thoughts may be, your awareness is much bigger than the pain.

Move your body before you sit: Take a walk or practice yoga or mindful movement before you sit to meditate. This will help to ground your attention to your body, and will in turn help your mind to focus on the present.

TENDING TO DOUBT

Spacious awareness: Doubt, like restlessness, can cause you to jump around from thought to thought, and from technique to technique. If you find you are experiencing doubt to the point where it is distracting, make space for doubt itself. Use that as your object of focus, without trying to find a solution or convince yourself that what you doubt is valid or not.

Commit to your practice: If you doubt your own skill or the practice itself, commit to a regular practice for a set period of time. For example, decide that you will meditate for five minutes every day for the next eight weeks, or 45 minutes a day for the next month. Set yourself up for success by committing to something manageable. Mark it on your calendar or set a reminder in your cell phone. Once you have finished this commitment, you can decide whether to continue your practice. Don't worry about the outcome, just think of it as an experiment.

Find a teacher: Join a mindfulness meditation group or *sangha* with a skillful teacher who instructs in the Buddhist *dharma*. This will help you to practice regularly, and learn how to overcome anything that gets in the way of your practice. It will also teach you that doubt is normal, and that the antidote is simply to keep practicing.

GRATITUDE VISUALIZATION

Suggested time: 15 minutes

This visualization is tailored for navigating the complex waves of grief. It's important to remember that this meditation is not about denying or diminishing the validity of your pain, but rather about finding a way to coexist with it.

Instructions

1   Find a comforting space to sit or lie down. Breathe in deeply, filling your lungs, and exhale slowly, releasing tension. Visualize a warm, comforting light surrounding you, creating a sanctuary of tranquility.

2   On an inhale, bring to mind something you are grateful for, visualizing it in detail. Let this gratitude spread throughout your body with each exhale, creating a warm, healing glow.

3   Visualize a supportive person in your life, experiencing gratitude for their comforting presence. Let this feeling spread throughout your body, and with each exhale, creating a warm, healing glow.

4   Visualize other people, objects, and resources for which you are grateful, no matter how small. Imagine a collage of appreciation, full of warmth, light, and resilience. Take a few moments to savor this image.

5   Bring your awareness back to your physical surroundings. Slowly wake your body and open your eyes.

6   In your journal, write a list of the sources of gratitude, the individuals, and associated feelings that came up during your visualization. This will be a tangible reminder, available anytime you need comfort and resilience.

MINDFUL JOURNALING: TRANSFORMING ROADBLOCKS INTO GREEN LIGHTS

Suggested time: 10–20 minutes

Follow the guidelines from Lesson 1 (page 32) to write in your journal. You may either use the guided exercise below, or write on your own.

Guided Journal Entry

Which of the Five Mental Hindrances do you encounter most often in your meditation practice? In your life? Use your journal to explore the physical manifestations of the hindrance and how it affects your relationship with yourself, your grief, and other people. What would be different in your life if you were able to transform this hindrance from a roadblock into a green light? Imagine having a conversation with the hindrance, and sending it loving-kindness.

LESSON 6
CONTINUING
BONDS

HONORING THE LEGACY
THAT REMAINS

*Don't let us half die with our loved ones, then;
let us try to live, after they've gone,
with greater fervor.*

SOGYAL RINPOCHE, *THE TIBETAN BOOK OF LIVING
AND DYING*

THE RELATIONSHIP LIVES ON

A loved one's physical absence is profound, like a jagged tear in the fabric of your existence. Compounding this pain is the erroneous advice from unhelpful sources that you need to "let go," or "move on," or "get back to normal," whatever that means. You would never want to forget your loved one, but you can learn to live with your loss, make sense of the incomprehensible, and find your meaning amidst the chaos. One way to do this is to embody what you already know: that your loved one was important, is still important, and will always be important.

CONTINUING BONDS

Your relationship does not end just because your person is not physically present. Outdated grief models emphasize detachment and "letting go" as a necessary part of healthy grieving and moving forward but, fortunately, modern grief models support what we know in our heart. The relationship with our loved ones does not die when they do. It continues to evolve and inform our worldview.

This ongoing connection—known as continuing bonds—is often cultivated through memories, sharing stories, internalized relationships, rituals, or even through objects that the deceased person valued or used (Klass, et. al, 1996). This perspective shifts the focus from "closure" and "moving on" to one of continuing connection and relationship. It provides a framework to support the idea that the deceased continues to play an influential role in the lives of those left behind, and that such connections can aid in the grieving process.

GRIEF AND DIFFICULT RELATIONSHIPS

Grief journeys are deeply personal. It's important to find the path that suits your unique situation and your attachment style to the person who has passed away. This becomes even more intricate when dealing with difficult relationships. Toxic, abusive, volatile, codependent, or unreliable connections can add layers of complexity to the grieving process. Even in healthy relationships, hurtful last words or acts can overwhelm positive memories.

With complicated relationships, reactions are not limited to what you might expect—such as sadness, anger, anxiety, guilt, for example—but can trigger conflicting emotions such as relief, emancipation, vindication, and even joy. Rather than feeling shame for very real feelings, this type of loss begs for self-compassion and understanding.

Continuing bonds can still provide an avenue for healing and personal growth. By acknowledging the intricacies of the relationship and allowing space for conflicting emotions, you create room for understanding and forgiveness. Despite the strain the bond may have endured in life, continuing bonds offer an opportunity to navigate unresolved emotions and foster a sense of peace and connection in the face of loss. This may involve revisiting memories, seeking support from others who can empathize, or engaging in introspective reflection to come to terms with the nuances of the relationship.

MEANING RECONSTRUCTION

Continuing bonds illuminate the enduring connection we hold with our departed loved ones, reminding us that their presence can transcend the boundaries of physical existence. Meaning reconstruction invites us to engage in the profound task of reshaping our understanding of the world and our place in it. Together, these intertwined concepts empower us to honor the past, find purpose in the present, and shape a future that embraces both the pain of absence and hope for our future.

For many of us, grief serves as a "wake-up call" that forces us to reprioritize the people and projects in our life. "By incorporating the reality of the trauma into our revised assumptive world and assigning it a personal meaning, we may be transformed by tragedy and made 'sadder but wiser' by the experience," Dr. Robert Neimeyer writes in *Lessons of Loss: A Guide to Coping* (2006). This process of reconstructing meaning helps us to carry on. There are two primary ways that we make meaning from our loss: by making sense of it and by finding benefit from it. Of the two, research indicates that making sense of the loss is the most helpful.

MAKING SENSE OF WHAT HAPPENED

Making sense means comprehending the loss in the most constructive way possible. For instance, if your loved one was in pain when they died or experienced a prolonged illness, it is natural to feel relief that their suffering is over. You may remind yourself that they are no longer in pain. In the case of military personnel, police, or firefighters, you may find comfort in acknowledging that they died for their country or while saving another person's life.

Of course, these two examples may not resonate with you at all. You wish they were still here, or that they had not placed themselves in danger: this is natural too. Remember that there is no right way to grieve, so the way you make sense of your loss must feel right in your own heart. If it feels like a dismissive platitude, it is not helpful and you should not force yourself to buy into anything you do not believe. Making sense may take time, and most of us achieve it eventually.

GROWTH AND GAIN THROUGH ADVERSITY

The process of making sense can bring a positive perspective to the loss—in discovering benefits, we identify the positive effects it has had on our personal existence. As Dr. Neimeyer suggests, we may be left "sadder but wiser," from a greater appreciation of the little things, to more affectionate relationships with family. Maybe you mastered a new skill, or marvel at your ability to sustain yourself despite the void left by your departed loved one. Tangible benefits like an inheritance in the form of money or property can be a potential positive aspect of loss, although this can elicit a myriad of complicated emotions.

Since you are working through this book, you may already realize that your empathy towards yourself and others has increased since your bereavement. This is a benefit. Undoubtedly, the majority of us would choose to have our loved one returned over finding meaning or benefits, but once we comprehend that the loss is irrevocable, it is natural to seek positivity. This search requires time and is a journey rather than a destination. The significance we extract may evolve numerous times throughout our lives, as our worldviews and beliefs shift with our experiences. Meaning reconstruction also encompasses the process of rebuilding our identities.

MEANING-MAKING AND UNEXPECTED LOSS

If the death is timely and somewhat expected, as in the loss of an elderly person, we will still feel sad, but we may not need to reorient our beliefs too dramatically. Understanding your experience of loss may be more difficult when the death is traumatic or unexpected, as in the case of suicide, homicide, or accident. We all want to believe that the world is basically a good place, but a violent or sudden loss may violate that assumption and challenge your ability to make sense of it all.

Dr. Neimeyer highlights the importance of rewriting our "self-narrative" after loss, especially when faced with fear or distressing images. In cases of violent or sudden death, professional help may be necessary, particularly if symptoms of PTSD arise. While a small percentage of people may experience complicated grief and require professional intervention, most of us can find meaning, rediscover purpose, and move forward without professional help.

• BONNIE'S STORY •

Martha was a professional chef who lived in a small town in rural Virginia with her husband, Rico, and her two children. In 2002, Rico died by suicide. Five years later, Martha ended her own life on the anniversary of her mother's death. She left behind a letter that listed her complaints. Reviewed one by one, each may have seemed manageable, but their sheer number was overwhelming.

Martha was one of five siblings, and her sister Bonnie was given the task of administering her estate to her children, Elizabeth and Robert. "It was a couple of years after she died before I started dealing with my grief. The estate gets disbursed over time, and we have seven years to go until the final payment is made," Bonnie said. "I think being the executor has put my grief on hold. I still feel like I have a job to do." It is not uncommon for administrative tasks, such as administering the estate, dealing with insurance, or legal proceedings, to delay the grief process. "Her daughter is still very disconnected with the family, and I think that is because we are all over the country. I live in Pennsylvania, so fortunately one of Martha's very good friends took Elizabeth in. She was in her mid-twenties when her mother died, and is almost 30 now. The friend wakes her up and makes sure she gets to work, and has her pay rent and fill normal adult roles. So she has someone who is taking care of her. She and her brother, Robert, are just now starting to talk about what happened, and that is helpful. Robert and I have an amazing relationship—not that I am a replacement for his mother—but we are really close. He even includes me in all his wife's and in-laws' events. I know that I am handling it very differently from my siblings, and I think that's because of my involvement with Robert."

When Bonnie and Robert cleaned out Martha's house, Bonnie found a stack of the beginnings of children's stories about cooking and kids. She told Robert that she would transcribe them one day, and got his permission to take them. It took Bonnie several years, but eventually she felt she could deal with Martha's books: "I made a Shutterfly book. I transcribed all her stories and scanned in some of her handwritten notes. At one point she had sent them to our dad, and he had critiqued them. He was the superintendent of schools, so there were the red markings of a teacher. I scanned those in, pictures, whatever was there. The main story was called Robert and the Radical Roast. Since they were all stories about cooking and kids, at the end you learned that you had to clean up your mess. And so every story ended with 'don't forget to clean up your mess!'"

Bonnie produced a hardcover version for Robert, and asked her siblings if they were interested in a copy. "I let them know I could send them a PDF of the book. I let them know it was not a big literary thing, but I asked them if they wanted to see Martha's work. My sister Erin told me that all she wanted for Christmas was a hardbound copy of that book."

When Christmas arrived, Bonnie watched Erin open the book and immediately push it aside. "It was like she wasn't expecting it, or like she felt it wasn't a Christmas gift. Her reaction was so quick to put the book aside that it hurt. I didn't say anything to her, but it is painful that they are still not able to talk about Martha. I don't want her to be forgotten."

Bonnie feels Erin has not yet come to terms with Martha's death in part because she feels guilty. Hours before her suicide, Martha got drunk and called Erin. Since it was the anniversary of their mother's death, Erin did not want to deal with the drama, and did not pick up the phone. She listened to the voicemail message, but did not return the call. "Erin is still struggling with that," says Bonnie. "I have some guilty feelings too, because we never addressed her problem with drinking. Instead of saying 'I can tell you are drinking, what's going on?,' I would say things like 'I'm just running out the door, can I call you tomorrow?' or I would call her in the early afternoon before she started. I tortured myself with the television show *Intervention* after that. For months I beat myself up, asking 'Why didn't I do that?'"

Both sisters ignored Martha's drinking problem, but Erin feels guilty while Bonnie has mostly let herself off the hook. There are two possible reasons for this difference. First, Erin is the person Martha called right before her death. If it had been Bonnie, the tables may have been turned. Second, Bonnie works in a mental-health facility and knows that even if she had staged an intervention for her sister, the chances of it succeeding would have been slim, and beyond her control. She knows that for change to happen, the person has to want it.

As you can see, we all mourn differently, even when we have the same biological relationship to the person who died. If you consider everyone in your own circle of grief, you probably recognize that each person has their own opinion about the person who died, and how that affects their worldview. It is not uncommon for some people to want to talk about the dead person while others can barely speak their name. This can change the dynamic of a family.

Bonnie wishes her siblings could talk about Martha, not just for themselves, but to help Bonnie with her own grief. She thinks it would be helpful to reminisce about the good times they shared. Unfortunately, their silence not only reinforces the fact that Martha is gone, but also seems to wipe out a portion of Bonnie's own past. While she understands that her sister feels guilty and that her brothers are angry that Martha committed suicide on the day reserved for celebrating their mother, the silence is driving a wedge into the relationships that remain.

Bonnie began practicing yoga two years after her sister died. She had gained so much weight that her health was at risk. "I began reaching out for things that I thought would help. It wasn't so much the yoga that I found helpful, because it made me feel uncomfortable because of my weight. I knew I had to stop what I was doing to myself. I had a few bad years, including Martha's death and other stuff that I had not handled well. I don't think Martha's death was the only thing I had to deal with, but working through grief helped me with everything else."

Bonnie saw a poster for my Mindfulness and Grief group in a yoga studio. For several weeks in a row, she shared with the group that she would see colors when she closed her eyes to meditate. She would spend the time mentally trying to arrange the colors into the order of the rainbow, but they would not budge. One night after class, she told me in an email: "My colors didn't make sense and I tried twice to rearrange them and make them flow in the right direction where yellow and blue would flow to green. They wouldn't change, so I stopped trying to change them. The breaths felt good, and they felt right, and they were beautiful, so maybe they were telling me that even though things don't make sense, don't give up: accept it, wonder about it, enjoy it, but don't try to change it."

Bonnie feels that she and Robert are adapting well to their loss because they are facing it, and making meaning out of a tragic situation by helping other people. They are very involved in community activities that raise awareness of and support suicide prevention. Every year since Martha's death they have participated in their local Out of the Darkness Community Walk, which is offered in hundreds of American cities to benefit the American Foundation for Suicide Prevention. One year they raised funds to travel and participate in the National Overnight Walk in Boston. Robert has even sat on a suicide survivor panel to help others to navigate their painful loss.

Bonnie is a grant administrator for a community mental-health provider, a job she had before her sister's death. "After she died I looked up what mental-health resources were available in her small town, and other than a once-a-week AA [Alcoholics Anonymous] meeting, there was nothing." Bonnie is able to make meaning through her day job, too, since the population she serves includes people with suicide ideation. Although she was not able to save her sister, she is able to save other people and to prevent their families from experiencing the pain her family now faces.

HONORING YOUR LOVED ONE

While not everyone has the opportunity to help others through their day job, you may find it beneficial to do something positive in honor of your loved one. Whether you contribute money or time to their favorite charity, rescue their favorite breed from a shelter, or volunteer for an organization that provided support through a long illness, there are countless ways that you can do something to help continue their legacy. This does not mean you are glad that they died; rather, it means you are grateful for the time you shared, and that you are willing to make the world a better place in their honor.

Some years after her sister's suicide, Bonnie continues to practice yoga, and organizes a weekly class at her local yoga studio that is open to all her coworkers. Physically, she is much healthier. She lost weight, and enjoys biking and running in charity events. This past year she got married. She still misses her sister, but both her relationship with her nephew Robert and her ability to help others transform her sadness into compassion.

Bonnie found several ways to make meaning from her sister's death, and while she feels she has not completely processed her grief, she is well on her way to a healthy adaptation, as meaning-making is one of the indicators of a successful grief journey. Let's review the many ways Bonnie has made sense of her loss:

- Established and maintains a positive relationship with her nephew Robert
- Volunteers for events that raise awareness of suicide prevention
- Practices Right Livelihood by performing a job that serves others and conforms to her values
- Produced her sister's book to share with the family and ensure her legacy
- Practices self-compassion by taking care of her own health.

If you review this list, you will see that Bonnie has taken a tragic and sad circumstance and found a way to help herself, Robert, and other people touched by suicide. It did not happen overnight. In fact, it has been a long journey, including a period of time when Bonnie numbed her grief through overeating. Now she approaches her grief mindfully. She attends to it, but does not become attached to it or try to deny its presence. As a result, she is able to extend compassion and loving-kindness to her family and all the people who her volunteer efforts support.

Although Martha has died, Bonnie still feels close to her sister in many ways. These continuing bonds are a reminder that although the person has died, the relationship remains, albeit in a changed state. This is an internal experience that for Bonnie exists as happy memories, and continues in the role she now plays in Robert's life. Unless an ongoing connection with the person who died prevents you from moving forward in the grief process, as with ambivalent, abusive, or difficult relationships, continuing bonds are normal, and provide comfort for most people.

LESSON 6 PRACTICE EXERCISES
Continuing Bonds: Honoring the Legacy That Remains

Mindfulness Meditation: Breath Awareness 45 minutes

Mindfulness Journaling: Life Imprint 20 minutes

Continuing Their Legacy: Varies

MINDFULNESS MEDITATION: BREATH AWARENESS

Suggested time: 45 minutes

Use the instructions from Lesson 1 (page 31) to practice seated mindfulness meditation with breath awareness.

MINDFULNESS JOURNALING: LIFE IMPRINT

Suggested time: 20 minutes

Inspired by the work of Vickio (1999) and Neimeyer (2016), this practice prompts you to reflect on your continuing bond with your loved one. In your journal, consider how your bond has influenced your personality, values and beliefs, and the many other aspects of your life, from education, work and hobbies to your style of communication, your view of yourself and other people, and even your unique mannerisms and gestures.

Which of these qualities do you want to nurture and carry forward in your life? Are there any behaviors you wish to release, transform entirely, or adjust?

CONTINUING THEIR LEGACY

Suggested time: Varies

There are many ways that you can continue your loved one's legacy while helping the planet and other people. Your activity can be public or private. You can plant a tree, volunteer at a school, walk to raise money, start your own charity, or plan an annual family gathering to honor your loved one's life and share their stories with future generations. There really are no limits to the ways you can establish continuing bonds and make meaning from your loss.

Instructions

Brainstorm ways to honor your loved one's memory. Altruistic efforts may bring comfort, but do not commit to any activity until you are ready. Consider this as a research project that you can implement now or at a later date.

LESSON 7
ALLOWING TRANSFORMATION

WHO AM I NOW?

When identification with the small sense of self drops away, what remains is the spacious heart that is connected with all things.

JACK KORNFIELD, *THE WISE HEART: BUDDHIST PSYCHOLOGY FOR THE WEST*

TRANSFORMING AFTER LOSS

Grief has changed you, chiseled into your being, and created a new version of you. But remember, change remains a journey, not a destination. Every moment brims with potential for evolution. Loss has peeled away familiar layers, leaving you raw. It's daunting, this undefined self, yet it's also a priceless opportunity, a blank canvas for you to tell a new story of resilience—that you can live with grief.

You also know that moments of triumph and stability can swiftly give way to waves of uncertainty and upheaval. As I shared in the first chapter, my ability to maintain equanimity amidst suffering stems from the observation that grief is a catalyst for transformative change. Rather than leave the shaping of your future self to the whims of fate, destiny, or happenstance, seize the reins of your own journey and steer it deliberately towards the path aligned with your deepest values and aspirations. So when you ask the inevitable question, "Who am I now?" consider who it is that you want to be.

• KEITH'S STORY •

Dillon was 31 years old and driving down one of the main streets in Washington, DC, when his eyes met those of an attractive, tan young man. Dillon was so intrigued that he made an illegal U-turn and pulled up alongside the 26-year-old Keith, who had just returned home from a trip to South America. The two hit it off immediately, and from that point on they were always together.

They bought their dream home, started their own business, and traveled the world. An affectionate couple, they regularly exchanged impromptu words of endearment whether they were working or passing each other in the hallway of their home. When Dillon died unexpectedly at the age of 69, Keith was devastated.

Experienced in Tibetan meditation, Keith was not new to mindfulness, but he had never before experienced the intensity of grief. He knew he wanted to use his mindfulness practice to reduce his suffering. Two weeks after Dillon's death, Keith sent me an email requesting a Phoenix Rising Yoga Therapy session, and shared a little about his loss with me. "We spent every minute of every day together," he wrote, "and had a mutual unconditional love for each other the entire 38 years we were together. He was my true and only love, my best friend. The last 17 days have been almost unbearable, and I am totally exhausted, overwhelmingly sad, lonely, and at times very, very anxious."

When I met Keith a few days later, we did not exchange many words. He just curled up in a fetal position on the mat, covered himself with blankets, and cried. I placed my hands on his back and felt the irregular rhythm of his breath through the back of his rib cage. From time to time, I imagined what his breath would feel like in my own body, a technique I use to establish an empathetic connection with someone and to anchor myself to the present moment. Touch can be very helpful when you are grieving, especially if you lost a spouse or partner. Every now and then, I guided him to focus on his breath, too. We stayed there for about an hour.

Each time Keith returned for a session, he was able to stay in the present moment a little longer. He explained how it helped him: "When you meditate, your mind wanders off after, say, one-millionth of a second, and then the next time you meditate you get to three seconds. Eventually you have more and more seconds each day where you are not in full grief mode. There is a point where you are so focused, you can choose the alternative to obsessing over your grief. For me, that was the beginning of 'this is how you are going to be.' My mindfulness practice was retraining my habits and showing me how to live without Dillon."

Keith and Dillon were so connected that they made every decision together. "Suddenly I was so alone, so totally lost. Even though I knew I was capable of making decisions, I had no confidence in myself. I didn't want to make decisions. I didn't want to move on." Seemingly small tasks felt overwhelming without Dillon: "I needed a repair man to come fix the doorbell. Normally, Dillon and I would have discussed it. I would say 'I need to get the doorbell fixed.' Dillon would agree. I would then call the repair man. But without him to validate my feelings, it took me six or eight weeks to make that call. Maybe it was habit more than the need for me to be validated. You have to learn to redo all your habits."

Mindfulness helped to ground Keith in the present and allowed him to look inside himself for answers, rather than outside, to Dillon. Mindfulness calmed his anxious mind. "The calming breath helped change my focus to think of now, and not two weeks from now. I could feel that right this very second everything is okay. Just feeling my back touching the floor slows me down. It takes the pressure off and reduces my anxiety." He also began to realize that he could grieve in his own time, and did not need to take advice from other people. "I realized I don't have to solve anything. I don't have to be grief-free within a certain amount of time. People would tell me 'It's been three months already.' They didn't have the slightest idea—in fact I didn't have the slightest idea what grief was like until I lost Dillon."

In spite of his grief, Keith is grateful that he and Dillon were able to have such a long and fulfilling relationship. "When Dillon died suddenly, there was nothing left unsaid between us. There were no regrets, and I wouldn't have lived my life differently."

Keith's transformation has been profound, and I am grateful that I have been able to witness his grief process. When I met him just two weeks after Dillon's death, he could barely breathe during our sessions, much less speak. A few months later he joined the Mindfulness and Grief group. I remember watching him during the yoga practice around week number four. He reached his arms in front of him and opened them wide, inhaling deeply. His eyes were closed and his face was soft. As he lifted his arms overhead I detected the faint hint of a smile.

Eventually Keith joined my regular weekly meditation group, which is open to the general public. He began to travel again on his own, visiting exotic lands for extended periods of time. His personal journey was full of ups and downs, as most grief journeys are, but he has emerged safely on the other side, and is able to smile and laugh as he remembers the man he loved and their 38 years together.

Almost five years after Dillon's death, Keith is beginning again. He and his partner, Brian, are in the process of buying their dream house on the other side of the country. Keith feels grateful that he has found love a second time, and that he is able to share his happy memories of Dillon with Brian. "I am grateful that I am able to make the best of my life and circumstances. Dillon's death taught me that impermanence is a wonderful thing, because the suffering is impermanent, too."

WHAT TO EXPECT AS YOU CONTINUE YOUR GRIEF JOURNEY

Adapting to your loss includes remembering the person who died, reconstructing your relationship, and finding a way to exist in the world without that person. There are many bereavement models that are empirically valid and sensitive to the individual nature of grief. As we have acknowledged throughout this book, research shows that while there is no "right" way to grieve, there are common tasks that contribute to a healthy grief journey.

Many people mistakenly believe that there are five stages of grief. This notion stems from a misinterpretation of Elizabeth Kübler-Ross's popular book, *On Death and Dying* (1973). Dr. Kübler-Ross deserves limitless gratitude for improving the quality of life of people who are dying. She revolutionized the way we talk about death as a society, and she advocated for dignity for the dying. However, her book was written about the dying patient, not the bereaved left behind. She herself never intended her five observations of the dying to be construed as a series of stages through which a bereaved person would move in a particular order. No scientific research has been able to support these five stages as a universal response to loss.

I cannot stress enough that the experience of grief is very personal. While we can make a list of common reactions that include thoughts, feelings, and cognitions, we know that no two people will have exactly the same story of love and loss. That is why prescriptive models of grief don't work. Fortunately, today's grief professionals have established some helpful task-based models that can help us to adapt to loss in a healthy way without forcing us to conform to an imaginary universal path.

THE FOUR TASKS OF MOURNING

One of the most recognized of these models is Dr. William Worden's "Four Tasks of Mourning." Dr. Worden's goal is to offer a bereavement model that empowers us during the grief process, and that doesn't prescribe a particular order or time frame. He also acknowledges that we each work through grief in our own way, but that it can be helpful to have a reference point to help us to orient ourselves during the most difficult of times. Dr. Worden's book, *Grief Counseling and Grief Therapy: A Handbook for the Mental Health Practitioner* (2009), is written for a professional audience, but most people find these tasks easy to understand. The Four Tasks of Mourning can be used in tandem with the principles of mindfulness and Buddhist philosophy, which I will outline on the following pages.

TASK 1:

TO ACCEPT THE REALITY OF THE LOSS

Acceptance of reality is a key component of mindfulness. When we sit down to meditate, our aspiration is to explore the nature of reality through our six senses. We observe the stories we create, and let them drop away so that we can come face to face with the present moment. When we delude ourselves, it leads only to suffering. Accepting reality—on an emotional and intellectual level—is also an important element of grief work. It may be helpful to know that this doesn't always come immediately, but it usually comes eventually. It is simply part of the process of adapting to your loss.

When we receive the bad news that someone we love has died, our first thought may be along the lines of: "That's impossible, I saw them just yesterday." If you have had this experience, know it is just your brain giving you a moment to collect yourself. You are searching for information that will deny something you don't want to believe. Mourning rituals, such as the funeral or memorial service, can help to address this, and eventually your intellect will understand that this person is no longer physically present, and you will realize that the loss is permanent.

Emotional acceptance may take a little longer than intellectual acceptance. Many bereaved clients have reported picking up the phone to call their loved one, only to remember seconds later that no one will answer. Some widows or widowers wake up in the morning and are surprised at first by the empty bed. For most of us, our emotions eventually catch up and are able to move past the first task. You may find yourself moving in and out of disbelief while you accommodate to this task, just as you move into and out of awareness as you sit in meditation.

TASK 2:

TO PROCESS THE PAIN OF GRIEF

Avoiding your pain will only prolong the process of your grief. If you suppress it, you risk developing physical complications, as we saw on pages 94–96 with Kate's story. The pain we experience from grief is the pain the Buddha spoke of when he taught the First Noble Truth. Suffering is what we add to our pain when we deny it or become attached to it. The Middle Path of mindfulness teaches us to observe our pain so that we can reduce our suffering.

Keith was able to face his pain through the Middle Path. He used skillful means to move back and forth between loss-oriented processes—figuring out how to make decisions on his own—and restoration-oriented processes—using mindfulness to create periods of "non-grieving." Once he recognized that his anxiety was rooted in worrying about the future, he chose to take action, which reduced his worry and eased his suffering.

One of the most important instructions for effectively processing the pain of your grief is not to let anyone tell you how to feel. Dr. Worden cautions against letting other people tell you that you don't need to grieve, or listening to platitudes that belittle your experience. Grief is a natural response to loss, and while your mindfulness practice may help you to mitigate some of that pain, be patient with yourself and know that it won't go away overnight.

Remember that self-compassion comes first, and that you can alternate between witnessing your pain and restoring your resources. Honor your vulnerability, but don't deny your strength. Instead, find balance and use skillful means to modify how you approach your grief.

TASK 3:

TO ADJUST TO A WORLD WITHOUT THE DECEASED

Dr. Worden explains that adjustment to your loss needs to happen on three levels:

External: The way the death affects your daily life. Our daily habitual patterns may prevent us from fully understanding the role our loved one plays in our life until after they are gone. You may have to learn how to balance a checkbook, raise children on your own, cook for yourself, or come home without the familiar greeting of your pet.

Internal: The way the death affects your sense of self. Initially, you may feel that your self-confidence is at an all-time low, as Keith did. If you lost a spouse or domestic partner, you may feel fractured, somehow less of a person. Your loss may lower your sense of self-efficacy, so that you feel as though you have no control over what happens to you. At times you may feel helpless, especially if you are unable to fulfill a role your loved one left vacant. As you learn new skills to manage your external world, and get to know yourself through mindful inquiry, you may arrive on the other side of grief with higher self-esteem than you had before your loss.

Spiritual: How the death affects your beliefs. Certain losses shatter our assumptive world, and beliefs that we once took for granted suddenly seem tenuous. For example, the belief that "people are basically good" will be shattered after a murder. The thought that "God is looking out for me and my loved ones" will be questioned after a devastating car accident. "My spouse will always be around to support our family financially" will no longer be true after the death of a husband or wife. When death is sudden, untimely, or traumatic, spiritual questioning is more common. When a death validates our assumptive world, such as the timely loss of an elderly person, spiritual adjustment may not be required.

TASK 4:

TO FIND AN ENDURING CONNECTION WITH THE DECEASED IN THE MIDST OF EMBARKING ON A NEW LIFE

How do you go on living when someone you love has gone? This is the question most people ask in the early days of grief. By now you know there is no single answer, but that your mindfulness practice and knowledge of these tasks will help you to accommodate to your loss in your own way. It is helpful to know that you will not sever all ties with the person who died; instead, you will find a new way to maintain a connection to that person.

The memories you have are already part of your life, and will not go away. You learn how to incorporate the narrative of your relationship into your life as you move forward, without letting that story be your only focus. If you can talk about the person who died with friends and family, it can be very helpful. Unfortunately, it is not uncommon for some to throw a wrench into this scenario. For instance, friends may not speak your loved one's name for fear of causing you distress, or they may avoid you because your loss reminds them that one day they will be in your shoes.

Bonnie, whose story appears on pages 111–114, still experiences this some years after her sister's death. None of her siblings will mention Martha by name. This is very frustrating and upsetting for Bonnie, who wants to honor her sister's memory and help Robert to feel connected to his mother.

Keith, on the other hand, is able to share his memories of Dillon openly with his new partner. He also has his own way of remembering Dillon. "The monks at the meditation center I attended always told Dillon that he was an incarnation of one of the Buddhist spirits of compassion. When I do my chanting in the morning, "ohm mani padme hum" allows me to embody that spirit of compassion, which is like embodying the heart of Dillon, but on a much bigger scale. It makes me aware of the bigger picture."

Keith is able to maintain a bond with Dillon through the chant. It reminds him of the compassionate and loving nature of their relationship, and allows him to extend that compassion and love to all beings everywhere. He has "emotionally relocated" Dillon's spirit from the physical world into the essence of the chant. This serves the additional purpose of meaning reconstruction, since he is continuing Dillon's legacy through loving-kindness. This chant is a reminder, but not a tether, and allows him to maintain the memory but continue to live his life after loss.

GRIEF REACTIONS THROUGHOUT YOUR LIFE

Grief is a process that does not have a specific end point. While the intensity of your pain will subside, you may experience a resurgence of grief from time to time for the rest of your life. This can happen at major life events, such as graduations, weddings, and funerals. Strong emotions may show up at certain times of the year, such as anniversaries, birthdays, and around the date the person died. Sometimes one of the six senses, such as the smell of spring in the air, a whiff of perfume, or the sight of the first snowfall of the year, will remind you of a time before your loss. "Even seeing a bottle of Tylenol on the grocery-store shelf will be a trigger, because it elicits memories of the deceased," explains Dr. Rebecca Morse, a professor of thanatology at George Mason University, Virginia. Seemingly small reminders can cause a big resurgence of grief even years later. You may wonder what it would be like if the deceased person were still there. Dr. Morse explains that "all these reactions are normal, and eventually you will be able to remember the happy memories you and your loved one shared without feeling overwhelmed with sadness."

Keith has successfully adapted to his loss, but, like most people, he experiences the occasional pang of grief. "I have a psychotherapist friend who told me that whenever the waves hit, to let them wash over me without letting them take me down. She told me the waves would eventually get smaller and smaller, and they did. They still show up occasionally, often unexpectedly. I am able to recognize the wave and say 'Oh, this is what's happening: afraid, sad.' Then I start the breathing. I learned that instead of being a victim of the waves I can just focus on my breath. Then I can reflect on the tide pools and learn from them."

This transformation will include your new self-identity and a new relationship with your lost loved one. Your choice to grieve mindfully has also taught you to embrace your inherent Buddha nature, which has always been inside you.

LESSON 7 PRACTICE EXERCISES
Allowing Transformation: Who Am I Now?

Contemplative Meditation: Who Am I Now?: 45 minutes

Mindfulness Journaling: Posttraumatic Growth and Change: 20–40 minutes

Empowering Action (Off the Cushion): Varies

CONTEMPLATIVE MEDITATION: WHO AM I NOW?

Suggested time: 45 minutes

This self-exploration is twofold. Firstly, it reaffirms your core foundations, aiding you in your journey with resilience and grace. Alternatively, it may highlight a need for change, prompting growth. Reflection allows for a bridge between your current and future self.

Instructions

1 Allow your eyes to softly close or gently fixate on a point ahead.

2 Start a body scan, from the top of your head downwards, as you count 10 breaths. Notice all sensations, pleasant, unpleasant, or neutral.

3 When you reach your feet, reverse your scan for another 10 breaths. Be conscious of your entire being in the present moment.

4 Connect with your vitality through breath and other sensations. Be attuned to what feels vibrant within your body now.

5 Observe the dance of sensations throughout your body. If a particular spot draws attention, let it. Don't seek to control or alter it.

6 Recognize any sounds from within your body as part of your unique existence. Notice your breath—its flow and rhythm.

7 If your attention wavers, return to your breath rhythm, starting anew. Allow all experiences to enter your awareness.

8 Shift focus to the observer part of you—the part aware of being conscious. Ask yourself, "Who is experiencing this moment?"

Written reflection

Use the below queries as seeds for contemplation in your journal. You do not need to answer them all, just pick one or two that you feel you can address in this moment:

- What does my heart yearn for?
- What purpose do I want to serve in life?
- What fills me with gratitude?
- What is my truth or beyond truth?
- Who am I in this moment?
- Who am I now?

Envision yourself as you are now or as you want to become. Identify a word that captures your essence and repeat it silently with each exhale. Self-reflection requires vulnerability, wisdom, and courage. Appreciate your engagement in this meditation. Place your hand on your heart and offer yourself comforting words.

MINDFUL JOURNALING: POSTTRAUMATIC GROWTH AND CHANGE

Suggested time: 20–40 minutes

Follow the guidelines from Lesson 1 (page 32) to write in your journal. You may either use the guided exercise below, or write on your own.

The prompts are specially crafted to help you navigate the transformation that often follows loss. Through the exploration of the five domains of posttraumatic growth outlined in the first chapter, these prompts will guide you to actively tend to things in your life you want to transform. For now, focus on one prompt per session so you can dive deep. You can come back to the remaining prompts on a different day.

Guided Journal Entry

Appreciation of Life and Everyday Moments: Describe a routine part of your day that you usually take for granted. How can you find beauty, joy, or value in this seemingly mundane moment?

Improved Relationships with Others (and Self): Think about a relationship in your life that could be improved. What are three things you could do to make this relationship stronger? If you were to improve your relationship with yourself, what would those three things be?

Sense of New Possibilities in Lifestyle and Interests: If you could completely reinvent your daily routine, what would it look like? Similarly, consider an interest or hobby you've never pursued because of fear, lack of time, or any other reason. What steps could you take to explore it?

Increased Personal Strength and Self-Reliance: Recall a situation in which you overcame a significant challenge. How did you navigate it and what did it teach you about your personal strength? Additionally, identify one area in which you would like to become more self-reliant and write down the steps you could take to achieve this.

Spiritual Change or Growth: Reflect on a recent event or period in your life that has affected your spiritual beliefs or practices. How has this experience contributed to your growth? What are some spiritual goals you'd like to set for the future?

EMPOWERING ACTION

Try a new activity—either something that you've always wanted to do or a new interest. Engaging in new experiences not only helps you to develop fresh skills, but also create new memories that can be comforting. If you feel anxious, physical activities can help to ground you. If you are lonely, attend an event where you have something in common with others. Sadness may be alleviated by an activity that brings even a small spark of joy. These new experiences can gently shift your perspective, helping you find moments of solace and growth amidst your grief.

- Eat at a restaurant with a cuisine you have never tried before
- Take a cooking, knitting, or yoga class
- Try hiking, biking, or tennis
- Go to the symphony, art museum, or bowling
- Attend a lecture at your local college or a book-signing at a bookstore.

LESSON 8
PERPETUAL
MINDFULNESS

LIVING FULLY WITH LOSS

*Neither a space station nor an enlightened mind
can be realized in a day.*

HIS HOLINESS THE DALAI LAMA, *HOW TO PRACTICE:
THE WAY TO A MEANINGFUL LIFE*

CONTINUING YOUR JOURNEY

The past seven themes and the day-long retreat have equipped you with powerful self-care tools that will help you meet each day with a greater sense of composure and calm, known as equanimity. If you continue to practice mindfulness through your grief journey and beyond, your body, mind, and spirit will bask in the joy and cope with the sorrow without ever losing sight of the Middle Path. This will empower you to live fully and without fear. Here, you will learn how to continue your mindfulness practice as you live your life after loss.

THE TWO ARROWS
AND THE THREE REFUGES

The Buddha wanted us all to understand that pain is inevitable, but suffering is optional. The First Noble Truth tells us that we will experience pain. The Second Noble Truth reminds us that we do not have to suffer. The Buddha shared a teaching to help us to understand these first two Noble Truths.

Imagine you are struck by an arrow. It hurts. Then imagine being struck immediately by a second arrow. That hurts even more. The Buddha explained that the first arrow is pain that cannot be avoided. The second arrow represents our reaction to the first. It escalates our pain into suffering.

Avoiding the sting of the second arrow takes practice. You must be awake when the first arrow strikes, so that you can choose to get out of the way of the second. This is why you have to commit to your mindfulness practice. The reality is that if you do not plan to practice, the chances are that you will not do it. If you do develop a mindfulness practice, the odds are that you will find you cannot live fully without it. The Buddha offered guidance for those who wish to commit to their practice, called the Three Refuges: the buddha, the sangha, and the dharma.

The *buddha* refers to our own Buddha nature—our own ability to be kind, compassionate, and mindful.

The *sangha* refers to a spiritual community that follows Buddhist principles.

The *dharma* is the true nature of reality, or the teachings of the Buddha.

As I mentioned in the preface to this book, you do not have to be a Buddhist to practice mindfulness, or to benefit from the Buddha's guidance. For instance, you can modify the concept of the Three Refuges to support your own spiritual practice. Your sangha may be a church congregation, synagogue, or a Compassionate

Friends group. The important thing is to remember that mindfulness is a practice. Much like a foreign language or mathematics, if you do not practice mindfulness you will more than likely forget how to use it when you need it the most. Of course you can always pick up where you left off, but if it is part of your daily life, you will live with much less suffering than you would otherwise.

CONTINUING YOUR MINDFULNESS PRACTICE

As you move forward, there will be longer periods of time between the waves of grief. Unlike the ocean tides, there is no chart for the highs and lows of loss, so prepare yourself for unexpected emotional weather with a consistent mindfulness practice. This will help you cultivate equanimity when you wake up heartbroken and sad, and also savor and appreciate the precious nature of life.

When you pay attention to your senses of sight, sound, smell, taste, touch, and thought, life becomes more vivid, rather like watching television in high definition. You will be more awake, and rather than walking around in a fog you will begin to see the beautiful details of life more clearly. Here are some tips to help you keep your mindfulness practice on track as you move forward.

CREATE A DAILY PRACTICE ROUTINE

You will get the most benefit from your mindfulness practice if you set a time every day to practice and stick to it. Research shows that 20 minutes a day for eight weeks or longer will have positive health benefits; but even five minutes a day will still give you a break from your stress. It is better to do a little each day than to practice for longer once a week.

Practicing in the morning will help you to start your day with a clear mind and an open heart, while an evening practice can help to calm you down and prepare you for restful sleep. Experiment to find out what works best for you. If you have only ten minutes a day, consider splitting it into two five-minute practices, one in the morning and one in the evening.

JOIN A MINDFULNESS COMMUNITY

Practicing meditation with a group of people has its own kind of energy. Can you imagine walking into a room where everyone has chosen to practice being still? Whether a community is made up of five or 200 people, the fact that multiple people are willing to find peace in the moment is inspiring.

A skillful teacher will help to keep you focused and inspire you to stay present. This is also a valuable resource when you need compassionate, non-judgmental social or spiritual support. You can usually find a meditation group at your local Unity Church or holistic health center. Your town may also have a Buddhist Meditation Center or Mindfulness Community.

KEEP WRITING IN YOUR MINDFULNESS JOURNAL

As you continue on your grief journey, and throughout the rest of your life, you will have insights that will help you to connect to your True Self. When you write continually in your journal without editing or judging the content, you will tap into your inner wisdom. As you clear away the clutter of your conscious mind, your Buddha nature will emerge on paper or on screen.

At the time, these insights may seem so big that you think you will never forget them, but, as Mark Twain said, "The dullest pencil is better than the sharpest memory." Writing in your journal will also help you to view your experience from a mindful distance. Many clients have told me that writing down their fears, bad dreams, and worries helped them to externalize the experience and then let it go.

CONTINUING YOUR GRIEF JOURNEY

Grief is a journey, not a destination. The suffering will become less and less intrusive and eventually will seem to fade away altogether. Then, one day, out of the blue, it will show up again. You will recognize it and know that you will survive. You may feel that to let go of your pain would somehow be a betrayal, a sign that you no longer love the person you lost. I hope the stories in this book have illustrated the fact that once you are able to relinquish the suffering, you will continue to love and remember the person you lost. Remember these tips from this guide as you go forward:

Mindful Awareness: Be present in the moment and treat whatever arises with compassion.

Conscious Relaxation: Allow your body to tap into the natural relaxation response.

Compassion and Forgiveness: Recognize that we are all interdependent and that all humans wish to be happy and free from suffering.

Skillful Courage: Alternate between restoring your resources and mindfully facing your pain.

Retreat: Every now and then enjoy a day of silence to be alone with yourself.

Getting Unstuck: Recognize distractions and attend to them with skillful means.

Continuing Bonds: Honor the enduring connection with your loved one..

Allowing Transformation: Determine who you want to become and mindfully reconstruct your identity.

Perpetual Mindfulness: Commit to a daily mindfulness practice and continue writing in your journal for lifelong equanimity and resilience.

LESSON 8 PRACTICE EXERCISES

Perpetual Mindfulness: Creating a Practice for Life

Relaxation with Choiceless Awareness 30 minutes

Mindfulness Meditation: Choiceless Awareness 45 minutes

Mindful Journaling: The Hero's Journey 45 minutes

Sharing Your Journey: Varies

RELAXATION WITH CHOICELESS AWARENESS

Suggested time: 30 minutes

It is important to remember that your mindfulness practice is about being, not doing. There will be periods in your meditation when you feel as though you are attached to a specific result. The practice of choiceless awareness will help you to relax and connect with the part of you that is awareness itself.

Take a moment now to ask yourself "What part of me is aware that I am reading this book? What is the part of me that sees?" You will come to realize that it is awareness itself. The wonderful benefit of this exercise is that it connects you to the part of you that is bigger than your pain, bigger than sadness, bigger than any one single experience. When you learn to take refuge in the part of you that is so expansive it can simply watch what happens, you will be free of suffering.

During this practice, you will allow your body to soften. You don't need to control anything; just watch your experience. Observe your thoughts, emotions, and sensations arrive, sustain, and then fade away. If you become overwhelmed with emotion, or get distracted in thought, remember that you can always return your attention to your breath. You may also wish to place your hand on the spot where you are feeling the emotion, and say to yourself: "This, too."

Instructions

1   Create a space on the floor where you can lie down. Use a yoga mat or blankets to soften the space.

2   Lie on your back with your legs draped over a rolled-up blanket or pillow.

3   Cover yourself with a blanket if you think you may become cool.

4   Let your arms rest by your side and allow your face to soften.

5   Briefly scan through your body and notice if there is anything you can do to make yourself more comfortable.

6   Turn your focus to your breath. Take a few three-part breaths (see page 27) and then allow your breath to be easy and effortless.

7   Set your intention for your practice.

8   Allow your awareness to dance between your senses as stimuli rise and fall. Give yourself permission to allow whatever you notice simply to be noticed. Rest in this experience for as long as you wish.

9   When you are ready to end the practice, roll onto your side and use your arms to press yourself up to a sitting position, then move into your mindfulness meditation practice.

MINDFULNESS MEDITATION: CHOICELESS AWARENESS

Suggested time: 45 minutes

Use the instructions from Lesson 1 (page 31) to practice seated mindfulness meditation. Connect to your breath to anchor in the present moment. Once you feel ready, let go of all technique and allow whatever arises in your awareness to show up, without trying to push it away or hold onto it tightly. From time to time you will recognize that you are "hooked" by a thought. When that happens, return your focus to your breath until you are ready to let go and experience choiceless awareness again. Repeat until your meditation time comes to a close.

MINDFUL JOURNALING: THE HERO'S JOURNEY

Suggested time: 45 minutes

Follow the guidelines from Lesson 1 (page 32) to write in your journal. You may either use the guided exercise below, or write on your own.

Guided Journal Entry

Set aside some time to read your Mindfulness Journal. Use sticky notes, colored pens, or pencils to highlight passages that stand out as significant milestones on your journey through grief. Record the answers to the following questions:

• Who are the characters in this story?
• Are there any themes or passages that stand out more than the others?

- What is the most significant change between your first and last entry?
- What do you think is your next step to help you to move forward in your journey?

SHARING YOUR JOURNEY

At the end of my Mindfulness and Grief groups, each person is given a period of time to share their most significant journal entry, drawing, or collage. Research indicates that sharing our stories and feelings of loss is beneficial both psychologically and physically, and it is a nice closing ritual for the group itself. Sharing helps to heal not only the person who is speaking, but also the person who compassionately witnesses the offering.

Each person gets a turn, and we all agree to stay silent unless we are the person sharing. This gives each person a chance to speak and be heard. By this point, most people in the group no longer see themselves as separate, but recognize that we are one in this human experience. You can create this sharing experience with a good friend, or with someone who has experienced the same loss as you.

As you open up and share your vulnerability and journey, the bond between you will deepen. That is why it is important to choose a person who you trust, and who will be able to let you speak and be heard for an extended period of time. Here are some examples, but don't feel limited by this list:

- Read an excerpt from the beginning and the end of your journal. Share what has changed and what has stayed the same. This also works for drawings and illustrations in your journal.
- Play a song or read a poem that is a metaphor of your grief journey, or relationship to the person you lost.
- Write a special journal entry that describes who you are now, or who you are in the process of becoming.
- Talk about a yoga pose that symbolizes where you are on the path.
- Discuss how your mindfulness practice has affected your body and your experience of grief. Draw two "landscape" images of your body of grief, one that illustrates your body before you began your practice and another that illustrates your body as it is now.
- Bring in an object that represents you, and an object that represents the relationship you have with your loved one. Discuss the symbolism of each.
- Share your aspirational collage. Explain the significance of each image, and how it relates to the future you hope to create.

AFTERWORD

CLOSING REFLECTIONS

From the ashes of grief the ground of love will be fertilized, your closed body will begin to open back up, and you will arrive changed, but intact, on the other side. In the beginning it may seem like an impossible journey, but through the practice of mindfulness you will advance step by step by tiny little step. One day you will awaken and realize you are *living* with grief.

You know that you do not need to pretend you are not in pain, but have the skills to tend to your suffering with skill and compassion. You have learned how to use relaxation techniques that will help you through these difficult times and will also keep your body healthy for years to come so that you can live more fully. You have discovered how a regular meditation practice can help you find peace and equanimity in this moment, without concern about the past or what is to come.

My greatest hope is that at some point you will find that just like everything else, pain is temporary. You do have the ability to find refuge in the present moment, even on what seems like the worst day of your life. Now that you've spent some time with this practice, I hope that like me, you will continue to incorporate it into your daily life.

It is only fair to acknowledge that there may come a day where you feel completely derailed, and it will seem like sitting down to meditate is just not possible. Even after running Mindfulness and Grief courses for several years, I must confess I hit a roadblock myself when my stepfather died of a pulmonary embolism soon after returning home from surgery. I had just pulled up to his house to deliver a prescription and I walked in on medics trying unsuccessfully to revive him. His best friend, who had driven my stepfather home from the hospital, had called them to the scene.

My stepfather was a photographer, following in the footsteps of his father, whose images graced the covers of *Life* magazine. I was in charge of the estate, and it was overwhelming. For a period of time—I don't know how long—I found it impossible to sit still. I didn't write at all. I knew mindfulness could help me, but I was so on edge I could not get quiet. I seemed to be waiting for the phone to ring with more bad news, which it did.

During the next few weeks, our beloved dog Brandy and my dear paternal grandfather died. My maternal grandmother fell, broke her hip, and seemed to lose her mind. I was in a state of bereavement overload, a response that may occur when you don't have time to process one loss before the next.

So there I was—the grief expert, meditation teacher, yoga therapy practitioner—unable to sit still. I decided to take up tennis. Not the style of tennis you see on television or that is played at a country club, but the hitting-balls-at-the-practice-wall by yourself kind of tennis. I was actually able to do this mindfully, and it helped. Since I had no prior experience, it helped focus my mind. It brought me back to my body. It released a lot of my nervous energy, and soon I sat back down on my meditation cushion to begin again. Tennis was a bridge to practice, or perhaps it was a practice in and of itself.

Eventually I picked up my stepfather's camera, and I learned how to use it. Although he never gave me a lesson, I think I picked up a lot just being around him. At first, photography was bittersweet. Now it makes me smile, and I think of how proud and surprised he would be. It is my way of staying connected to him, while creating beauty in my own and others' lives.

My point in telling this story is to share with you that no matter how you choose to be with your grief, or live your life from this point forward, mindfulness is always an option. Sometimes it shows up as tennis. Sometimes, as photography.

Mindfulness is a powerful gift. I have experienced it for myself firsthand, and I have seen it work again and again in my online grief support program, Awaken (meditationforgrief.com). Writing this book has been a blessing, because I have had the opportunity to reconnect with several participants of my early Mindfulness and Grief groups. Each person I interviewed is still practicing mindfulness in one form or another. Some meditate regularly. Others do yoga. A few continue to keep a journal. Each person, however, was able to speak about their loved one with ease, laughter, and humor. This may take time for some but will come quickly for others. It is true that many grief books overlook the importance of levity, and so I will leave you with this thought:

Every now and then, remember the happy times you shared with your loved one. Just as you do not need to deny your pain, remember you do not need to deny your joy either. Do not be afraid to smile, and remember that laughter lets the light into our hearts.

May you be happy, as I wish to be happy
May you know peace, as I wish to know peace.
May you be free from suffering, as I wish to be free from suffering.

REFERENCES AND FURTHER READING

Benson, H., and Klipper, M.Z., *The Relaxation Response* (Avon Books, 2000)

Bonanno, G.A., *The Other Side Of Sadness* (Basic Books, 2009)

Brach, T., *Radical Acceptance* (Bantam Books, 2003)

Brach, T., "RAIN: Recognize, Allow, Investigate, Nurture," retrieved from tarabrach.com/rain

Calhoun, L.G., and Tedeschi, R.G., *Handbook Of Posttraumatic Growth* (Lawrence Erlbaum Associates, 2006)

Chödrön, P., *When Things Fall Apart* (Shambhala, 2000)

The Dalai Lama and Hopkins, J., *How To Practice* (Atria Books, 2003)

The Dalai Lama, *The Compassionate Life* (Wisdom Publications, 2003)

Doka, K., *Disenfranchised Grief* (Jossey Bass, 1989)

Doka, K.J., and Martin, T.L., *Grieving Beyond Gender* (Routledge, 2010)

Faulds, D., *Go In and In: Poems from the Heart of Yoga* (Morris Publishing, 1997)

Hanh, T.N., *Anger: Wisdom For Cooling The Flames* (Riverhead Books, 2002)

Kabat-Zinn, J., *Wherever You Go, There You Are* (Hyperion, 2005)

Kalss, Silverman, and Nickman, *Continuing Bonds* (Routledge, 1996)

Kornfield, J., *The Wise Heart* (Bantam Books, 2009)

Kübler-Ross, E., *On Death and Dying* (Routledge, 2008) 40th anniversary edition

Lee, M., *Phoenix Rising Yoga Therapy* (Health Communications, 1997)

Levine, S., *Unattended Sorrow* (Rodale, 2005)

Neff, K., *Self-Compassion* (William Morrow, 2011)

Neimeyer, R.A., *Lessons Of Loss* (Center of the Study of Loss & Transition, 2006)

Goldberg, N., *Writing Down the Bones* (Shambhala, 2005)

Rinpoche, S, Gaffney P, and Harvey A., *The Tibetan Book Of Living And Dying* (HarperCollins Publishers, 1993)

Rogers, J. E., *The Art Of Grief* (Routledge, 2007)

Rūmī, J, and Barks, C., *The Essential Rumi* (Harper, 1995)

Salzberg, S., *Open & Expansive* (Tricycle, 2009)

Stang, H., *From Grief to Peace* (CICO, 2021)

Steffan, Milman, and Neimeyer, *The Handbook Of Grief Therapies* (Sage, 2023)

Stroebe, M.S., and Schut., "The Dual Process Model of Coping with Bereavement," *Death Studies*, 23, pp. 197–224 (1999)

Treleaven, D.A., *Trauma-Sensitive Mindfulness* (Norton, 2018)

Worden, J W., *Grief Counseling And Grief Therapy* (Springer, 2009)

Every effort has been made to trace all copyright holders. Any omissions will be included in future editions if the publisher is notified.

RESOURCES

WHERE TO FIND SUPPORT

Use these resources to connect with a grief professional or support group.

Phoenix Rising Yoga Therapy Practitioner Directory pryt.com

Association of Death Educators & Counselors adec.org

National Hospice and Palliative Care Organization caringinfo.org

The Compassionate Friends: Supporting Family after a Child Dies
compassionatefriends.org

American Association of Suicidology suicidology.org

Suicide Prevention Lifeline 1-800-273-TALK (8255)

Open To Hope: Finding Hope After Loss opentohope.com

The Dougy Center dougy.org *Support for children and teens*

MISSFoundation: a Community of Compassion and Hope for Grieving
Families missfoundation.org

TAPS: Tragedy Assistance Program for Survivors taps.org *Support for
military loss*

National Fallen Firefighters Foundation firehero.org

Concerns of Police Survivors nationalcops.org

The Samaritans samaritans.org / 113 123 (UK and ROI)

CRUSE Bereavment Care cruse.org.uk and crusescotland.org.uk

USEFUL WEBSITES

Access mindfulness teachings through articles, podcasts, and events.

Mindfulness and Grief mindfulnessandgrief.com

Insight Meditation Community of Washington, DC imcw.org

Deer Park Monastery deerparkmonastery.org

Pema Chödrön Foundation pemachodronfoundation.org

Be Mindful bemindful.co.uk

Telesangha telesangha.com

RETREAT CENTERS

Learn more about mindfulness, find a sangha, or schedule a retreat.

Shambhala (International Directory) shambhala.org

Spirit Rock Meditation Center spiritrock.org

Insight Meditation Society dharma.org

Kripalu Center For Yoga & Health kripalu.org

Omega Institute eomega.org

INDEX